S0-BEV-211

REMEMBER ANONYMOUS BOSCH, GERMANY'S UNKNOWN SOLDIER, AND LOIS CARMEN DENOMINATOR, THE MATH TEACHER?

They're both to be found in this brilliant collection of over 700 entries from the zaniest contest ever!

"I am devoted to the book and the author, and next to *The Brothers Karamazov* found it the most important piece of literature any Russian writer has produced."
—Woody Allen

"Mary Ann Madden's book is bright, perceptive, sensitive, witty, topical, socially relevant and, mainly, I'm in it a lot."
—Dan Greenburg

"We love Mary Ann Madden's book."
—Betty Comden and Adolph Green

"Glittering, erudite parody, shameless burlesques, puns and spoonerisms . . . A picnic of delightful buffoonery fit for any palate."
—*Kirkus Review*

This anthology is humbly dedicated to me,
without whom
Stephen Sondheim
Wrote *West Side Story*, *A Funny Thing Happened
on the Way to the Forum*, *Anyone Can Whistle*,
Company, *Follies*, and thought up the whole idea of
doing competitions in *New York Magazine*.

—M.A.M.

Thank you for the Giant Sea Tortoise

you're welcome

and Other Unforeseen
Results of

New York

Magazine Competitions

MARY ANN MADDEN

LANCER BOOKS ■ NEW YORK

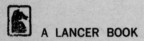

A LANCER BOOK

THANK YOU FOR THE GIANT SEA TORTOISE

This Lancer edition is published by
arrangement with The Viking Press, Inc.
Its large sale in the high-priced
hardcover edition makes possible this
inexpensive reprint.

LANCER BOOKS, INC. • 1560 BROADWAY
NEW YORK, N.Y. 10036

Table of Contents

Table of Contents

☞ *Introduction*

You may already be aware that this is a collection of the results of select *New York Magazine* Competitions. That's what it is, all right, and make few mistakes about it. If you're not interested in a collection of the results of *New York Magazine* Competitions, stop right here. Browse. If you don't see what you want, ask for it. On second thought, you might glance at this book of wide and multiple authorship, look for your friends' names, that sort of thing. But you don't have to *buy* it. Save yourself. Never mind about me. However, should such a compendium arouse you, dear aesthete, read on.

"Thank You for the Giant Sea Tortoise" was an entry to the "Unusual Greeting Cards for Unlikely Occasions" Competition from Tom Morrow of N.Y.C. Mr. Morrow is one of a passel of prodigiously regular contributors to these contests and a frequent winner of same, with others like Herb Sargent, Dan Greenburg, Miles and Judith Klein, Peter Stone, Carol Drew, and Henry Morgan to name too many.

Some of these competitors are professional wordsmiths, which might seem to give them an edge. It does. But this fact did not and does not discourage the faithful in their often successful bids to unseat these smarty pantses. An average of fifteen hundred entries are received by *New York* each week and then sent on to me in two batches. (The second drop accommodates only out-of-town postmarks by extending deadlines.) Then comes the fun. I read them. All. Alone. My elfin grot is inundated with stacks of entries designated "Stupendous," "Terrific," "Adequate," "Repeat—Save for Double Credit," and "Space Permitting." The "Repeat" pile bears bitter fruit. It's not unusual to receive as many as thirty verbatim entries of, let us say, "Shirley and Telephone Booth." But it's downright uncanny to unleash eight or nine "Under A and John Cheevers." This kind of duplication accounts for my outcast state. One simply has to remember what one's seen before (just like in the movies), and that is a solitary task. It gets lonesome but it's a living.

I guess people assume that thinking them up is the hard part. Wrong. It's the endless reading and sorting. And deciding. (Use of the actual brain itself is taxing, don't you find?) And awarding prizes. This is especially agonizing when one-liners are involved. You can spot a good parody without too much trouble. Assaying the relative merits of single double-entendres isn't a fountain. Sometimes *none* of them seems funny on the fourth or fifth reading. (It's tough to be alone on the shelf.) Sometimes you call a guru for an opinion. Sometimes no one agrees with your choices. (It's worse to be in love by yourself.) And so it goes. Or went.

For this collection, the task of editing was a somewhat different one. Entire competitions were eliminated as being either too parochial (limericks on the N.Y.C. mayoral race, for example), or of limited appeal (as in anagrams of *New York*'s advertisers). Reports of results were abbreviated: where applicable, they consist only of a refined list of "repeat" submissions. Prize-winners are not so designated, although entries do appear in their original order. Here, as in the magazine, there's an attempt to prevent a diminution of quality. After the first five or six results, you will find the sublime scattered among the swine, so to say. Credits for nonverbatim duplicates are not included because, well—for neatness' sake. What is left? Thirty-two spiffy contests cum results,

Plus—and N. this B.—MANY EXTRAS THAT LIM-ITED MAGAZINE SPACE DID NOT PERMIT.

Who enters? Professional writers, as I said, and free-(and, it would seem, often liberal-) thinking students, actors, copywriters, teachers, housewives, locksmiths, doc-tors, lawyers, alas, not too many Indian chiefs. But then you can't always tell by the letterhead. You *can* tell some-thing from the postmarks. Naturally, most are from the New York area, but an inspiring number come from all parts of the country and occasionally overseas. The all-time high mail counts were the "Odd Couple" and "Free Association" (Dan Greenburg) competitions; over nine thousand each.

"Why," you may ask, *"Thank You for the Giant Sea Tortoise?"* Well, why not? The business of title selection proved more staggering than strong drink, and nearly caused a schism between The Viking Press and the hapless undersigned. Alan Williams, editor, philologist, and cur-able romantic, wanted to call it *I Liked Being a Virgin Better, She Said* (an entry to a competition of "First Lines of Novels Destined for Oblivion"). This beguiling if not entirely credible title terrified me. Whereupon the follow-ing telephone conversation actually took place. Only the names are changed to protect the reader. "How about calling it *Pâté, Maison, and LaVerne?*" I offered. "Or, *I Never Rang for My Father?*" Other initial-letter rhymes for *"Sang"* were dismissed as ignoble. *I* was dismissed as ignoble.) "What do you think of *Guess Who Coming to Dinner? Or Anonymous Bosch—Germany's Unknown Soldier*—or—well, how about *Moby Dick* or *The Scarlet Letter* or *Nancy Drew and the Secret of Santa Vittoria?*" "Nothing." "Oh hell. C. P. Snow already has all the good titles anyway. Hey! How about *that?* How about calling it *C. P. Snow Already Has All the* . . . Hello? Alan? Hello?"

Well, there are a million stories in the naked city and

you've probably heard all of them. So if I tell you I'm going to call a book *Thank You for the Giant Sea Tortoise,* you'll just have to be a good sport about it. And another thing. Don't ask so many questions.

What else can I tell you? Oh, yes. The Competitions are based on the far more esoteric Oxford-donnish British competitions as in *Punch* and *New Statesman.* The idea to do them for *New York* sprang from Stephen Sondheim, composer–lyricist–games maven. His puzzles* appeared weekly in the magazine, but needing time to work on a musical, he switched to one a month and suggested the Competitions as an alternate feature, with me as possible editor. Brave, loyal, and reverent, Clay Felker, *New York*'s editor, took a chance. And the rest is nonfiction.

So, a series of grateful acknowledgments: to *New Statesman* for the concept on which these Competitions were generally (and in a few instances, specifically) based; to Steve Sondheim and Clay Felker, of course, and to Gloria Steinem for affording me the opportunity to do the Competitions for *New York;* to the indefatigable readers who entered them; to Burt Shevelove, who thought a book could be made of them; and to Tom Guinzburg, who published it and who spells his name so cute.

If, as I hoped, you are interested in results of *New York Magazine* Competitions, you ought to *love* this book. You really should think about buying it. Anyway, you've got a nice day for it. Peace.

—M.A.M.

* These sadistic puzzles are now executed by Richard Maltby, Jr.

*Thank You for the
Giant Sea Tortoise*

☞ I Went on a Long Trip

I went on a long trip. Buzz and Mike went too. No girls or pets or parents allowed but there still wasn't all that much to do like swimming. You have to wear a uniform and a hat the whole time and the food was boring. I guess it was O.K. if you like sight-seeing. You can kick the moon dirt with your toe. We took some swell pictures. I lost my good camera. Everybody made a big deal when we got back. Nèxt year I'm either going to Mars or getting a paper route.

Above, a composition by Neil Armstrong, age ten. Competitors were invited to submit an essay on this topic by a famous fifth grader.

I've given this awesome but inspiring project a great deal of thought and I believe that I am at liberty to tell of the experiences I had this summer. That is, if it is a composition about this current summer that is required. . . . I am more than willing to write about summer vacation, but, after further study of the assignment, I take note of the fact that no particular summer has been specified. I would not wish to jeopardize my standing by writing about the wrong summer. But then "wrong summer" is a defeatist term and I have not intended to apply it in the context of a summer, a summer in America, being wrong. More correctly, all of our summers are right. In terms of this composition, it would be difficult to commit myself to just any random right summer until I have prepared myself further as to which right summer is right. May I confer with you after class?   —R. M. NIXON

Barba DelPeard, Highland Park, N.J.

I wrote a story this summer because I like to make things up. But my teacher, Miss Leighton, says you should write about what you know so I wrote about my friend Jackie. She thinks she's so special but I know better. She always spends her whole allowance as fast as she gets it and she gets lots more than I do even though I'm just as good as she is and she's always whispering secrets to her dumb sister in the corner and she isn't nice to her mother and she's got a collection of silly old things that I would never save and she always wants new clothes and her dresses are too short because she's not a baby but she talks like one and she says when she grows up she's going to be the Queen of America and her sister will be a princess and she never wants anybody to know I'm her friend. And I decided that now that she's in school in Greece I could tell. Anyway I've got a new friend. Her daddy's a publisher.   —MARY BARELLI

Maureen Myers, N.Y.C.

First I went on our yat. Then for a ride on one of our planes. Then I went to one of our ilands. Then the yat. Then on another one of our planes. Then to one of our manshuns. Then another plane. Then the boring yat again. Then to another manshun. Another plane again. The dumb yat again. I wore my big earrings a lot on the yat. And I got a whole lot of new clothes.

—JACQUELINE ONASSIS

Eve Merriam, N.Y.C.

I walked myself on the ocean. I said, One must have light. *Alors,* there was light. *Très bien.* I made the sky. *Ensuite.* I took all the water and put her in the same place. I named earth that which was not covered. *Encore bien.* I made the stars, the sun, and the moon. I made the plants and the animals. I made a man. What a type! He looked just as me. Then I made a woman. Oo-la-la. *Enfin.* I am finished and I rest myself. Next summer, *peut-être,* I will give commandments or make floods.

> —CHARLES DE GAULLE
> *Norton J. Bramesco, N.Y.C.*

This year I vent to visit my aunt Vilhelmina in Stockholm. The veather vas varm, but at night it became chilly. My aunt bought me a pair of sandals that vas so large that the shoe clerk did not have a box to put them in and so I vore them home. They are vhite. I also saw my first movie film vhich is a lot of silly people on a large screen and no sound. My aunt told me this vas the vay these people make their living. Amazing! The trip home after my visit vas the most enjoyable part of my vacation since I traveled by train and I had a compartment all to myself.

> —GRETA GARBO
> *Kenneth Geisert, Ridgewood, N.Y.*

Camp was really rotten this year. The food was bad, the bunks were terrible, and no one knew how to play baseball right. It rained every day, so we had to stay inside (and that was rotten). Inside we saw all kinds of movies. King Kong was terrible in *King Kong Escapes.* No style. Snow White was an idiot in *Snow White and the Seven Dwarfs,* and Carroll Baker was the worst person in *The Carpetbaggers.* Since we were inside all summer, the kids put on a lot of plays. I saw *Peer Gynt,* which I hated, four plays called *A Black Quartet,* most of which I hated,

The Three Sisters (I hated it), *Black Electra* (I hated it),
Oedipus (ditto) and *Twelfth Night* (you guessed it—I
hated it). . . .
        —JOHN SIMON
Michele Ingrassia, Flushing, N.Y.

I went fishing. I caught some fish. The captain of the fishing boat caught a big white fish. We called it Mopey Dick
because it moped around a lot and was hard to catch. Ha!
Ha! The captain got killed. I got wet. I was in this accident and lost all my souveneers and my schoolbooks. My
folks were mad and said I have to stay home next summer. Fishing isn't all that great I decided. Neither is New
Bedford.
        —HERMAN MELVILLE
Eleanor Edelstein, Santa Monica, Calif.

On my summer vacation I took up saling. It was very
nice. Our scout troop got together and a very nice lady
contributed three boats so we could all earn our badges.
Sometimes it was very windy and we got sick. Then the
wind would fall off but the boats never did. I was made
captain and I was very stern (joke!). When it would be
stormy and the other boys wanted to chicken out and
tack home I would yell "Ceylon! Ceylon!" to boy up their
spirits and pretty soon we got there. I think.

        —CHRISTOPHER COLUMBUS
Mrs. Edward W. Powell, Jr., N.Y.C.

Two things happened this summer. First I caught the
chicken *Pox*. Then I caught a wild red *Fox* and kept him
in a *Noxon Box*. He must have been a Jewish *Fox* 'cause
all he liked was *Novi Lox*. He also chewed up Leon's
Sox.
        —DR. SEUSS
Carol Drew, Palisades Park, N.J.

There was this white tower in the Lake of Innisfree and
my friends Maud and Leda and Crazy Jane and me
played there. I loved watching the dolphins best, but

Leda and this swan became really good friends. Crazy Jane was always going off with this bishop. We danced and danced til we broke the marble pavement, but this lady named Gregory said she'd pay for it if I'd be her friend. Next summer I want to drive past Ben Bulben on a horse.   —W. B. YEATS
Stephanie Gold, N.Y.C.

I stayed home this summer. I have beautiful new house. Is white with big lawn and trees. I got elegant new desk and chairs. Nice reporters come to play and we sit around. Here everybody nice to me. I like. Town has colledge and tigers. Real tigers come from India. I had a friend from India but he died. Then I went on a long trip. I left my dolls and everything in Moscow but I took notebook with my story. I know English good now so I start learn French. Maybe will go there. I wrote new story. People give money to me for stories. I tell my adventures. I tell of Papa and Mama and men who worked for Papa. I tell Papa not crazy when they said he was.

                                    —SVETLANA ALLILUYEVA
Joanna Steichen, N.Y.C.

We moved. Me and Ham and Japheth and Mama and Papa and our pets which there's to many to name. We went in the boat Papa built. I thought it would be fun but it wasn't. The boat was to small and it has little holes insted of windows and we couldn't even go on the deck because of the lousy weather. I wished I was a penguin but I was only a kid and I had to keep cleaning up after the pets. It was offal.   —SHEM
Arnold Cover, Sarasota, Fla.

Some of my friends and me went on a sleep out on Uncle Max's farm. We camped in the field. It rained a lot but we got to go swimming. At night we sat around a grass

fire and sang songs. There were no horses so we had to
eat the sugar cubes we brought. It was a swell trip.

—ABBY HOFFMAN
Ann Baldwin, Merrick, N.Y.

Mater and Pater sent me and my sister, Berenice, to
Rome. It was interesting but they are not civilized like us
and we couldn't play with the kids there because nurse
says they are too rough. But Berenice made friends with
lots of soldiers and they took her places I wasn't allowed
to go because I am too young. They promised to write
but I don't believe that they can. Berenice invited them to
visit us next summer but I know they won't be let in the
palace. We saw a few carnivals and did some shopping
and when we got home we poisoned some slaves.

—CLEOPATRA
Dennis Johnstone, N.Y.C.

I had to go with my parents to Balmoral. Its a crumby
place. They don't have any gaurds changeing. There's a
lot of tree's and rivers there. But everybody doesn't visit
there like in London. Aunt Louise came to see us. She
always has to kiss me. I went fishing with my brother
George, he caught a trout. Its in Scotland. Its the most
terrible castle I've ever seen. There was one nice thing.
We had a bagpipper and he skirled every day. I think you
could have a better time some place else. It was a good
place for my sister. She likes to embroider. Maybe you
could have a good time in America. I'm glad to be back
in London.   —EDWARD ALBERT CHRISTIAN GEORGE
ANDREW PATRICK DAVID WINDSOR
James Fechheimer, Glen Head, N.Y.

☞ *Dean Martin and Jim Brown in . . .*

Dean Martin and Jim Brown in *The High and the Mighty*

Rock Hudson / Cliff Robertson / Craig Stevens /Rudy Vallee in Ivan Tors' Production of *The Magic Mountain* **with Steven Hill/Grover Dale/ Joan Rivers/Donald Woods/Gabe Dell/Jayne Meadows and Miss Peggy Lee.**

Above, actual films with recouched casts. Competitors were invited to submit film titles with appropriate casting suggestions.

Repeats: A Man For All Seasons with Shelley Winters/ Elke Sommer/Spring Byington
Royal Wedding with Alan King / Steve McQueen / Patty Duke/*et al.*, directed by Harold Prince (occasionally including *The Cardinal* with Joey Bishop/Charles Chaplin/ *et al.*, by J. B. Priestley)
Finian's Rainbow with Pinky Lee/Joel Grey/Ben Blue/ *et al.*
The Apartment with Diana Dors/Evelyn Keyes/Clark

* Repeats: A list of typical entries. Good, but duplicated in quantity too great for individual ascription.

Gable/*et al.* (also appearing in *The Fixer* with James Mason/Gary Cooper/Christopher Plummer/*et al.*)

The Good Earth and *On the Beach* with Tommy Sands/Blossom Dearie/Natalie Wood/Mary Astor/*et al.*

The Zoo Story and *The Birds* with Max Baer/Sue Lyon/Walter Pidgeon/George Segal/*et al.*

Ice Station Zebra (Raymond Burr), *A Christmas Carol* (Yul Brynner/Noel Coward). Also-rans: Howard Hughes in *The Invisible Man*, Charlie Chan in *I Am Curious (Yellow)*, and endless trios of *The Good, the Bad, and the Ugly*

Fay Wray/Alvino Rey/Ray Milland/Gene Raymond/Johnny Ray/Sugar Ray Robinson/Martha Raye/Ina Ray Hutton/Ray Danton/Raymond Burr in *As Thousands Cheer* with Hoot Gibson

Isabel Jeans and Joseph Cotten in *Blue Denim* with Red Buttons

Fred Cline, N.Y.C.

S.P. Eagle Presents *The Awful Truth* starring Margarita Cansino/Dino Crocetti/Tula Ellice Finklea/Sarah Jane Fulks/Greta Gustafsson/Phyllis Isley/Doris Kappelhoff / Archie Leach / Lucille LeSueur / Shirley Schrift / Ruby Stevens

Howard Haines, N.Y.C.

Hurry Sundown starring Barbara Rush and Race Gentry with Frank Gallop as Eddie Cantor/Skip Homeier as Willie Hoppe/Robert Walker as Eric Ambler/Sp. Guest Star Fredric March/Written by Speed Lamkin/Additional Dialogue by Howard Fast/Costumes by Don Loper/Music by John Scott Trotter/Produced and Directed by David Swift

Cornel Wilde/Alan King/Dom de Luise in *Wild Kingdom*

Buster Crabbe and Groucho Marx in *Repulsion*/Written by Kenneth Anger/with Titus Moody as George Meany/Produced and Directed by Sidney Furie

Herb Sargent, N.Y.C.

A Tree Grows in Brooklyn with Stephen Boyd and Earl Holliman

Anthony Perkins, N.Y.C.

Anthony Dexter in *Great Expectations* with John Agar/Edmund Purdom

David Fractenberg, New Paltz, N.Y.

Elizabeth Taylor/Eli Wallach/Joanne Woodward/Richard Burton / Anne Jackson / Richard Benjamin / Paula Prentiss/Paul Newman in *Couples*. Also Starring Jack Lemmon and Walter Matthau

Arnold Cover, Sarasota, Fla.

Butterfly McQueen/Arthur Treacher/Eddie Anderson in *Help!*

Nancy Salz, N.Y.C.

Barbra Streisand IS *"Hud"*

Milton Tatelman, N.Y.C.

James Mason/Pamela Mason in *House of Strangers*

Marcia Savage, Corona, N.Y.

Debbie Reynolds/Elizabeth Taylor/Connie Stevens in *The Shoes of the Fisherman*

Phyllis Honey, N.Y.C.

Princess Margaret Rose in *Charley's Aunt*

> Robert Moberly, N.Y.C.

Leon Bibb and Forrest Tucker in *Top Hat*

> Bunny Stivers, N.Y.C.
> Dion McGregor, N.Y.C.

Hal Roach Presents Franz Kafka's *Metamorphosis*

> David Martin, N.Y.C.

Henry Fonda in *Whatever Happened to Baby Jane?*

> Jim Saslow, Princeton, N.J.

Duke Ellington and Joe Valachi in *The Cat and the Canary*

> Nat Brooks, Flushing, N.Y.

Barbra Streisand in *Rear Window*

> Robert and Susan Sekuler, Evanston, Ill.

Joseph McCarthy in *The Russians Are Coming! The Russians Are Coming!*

> Donald Wigal, N.Y.C.

Norman Wisdom and Kitty Carlisle in *The Owl and the Pussycat*

> Ted Cordes, Hollywood, Calif.
> Michael D. Parsons, N.Y.C.

The Lady Vanishes starring Maria Callas

> Barbara Walker, N.Y.C.

Isobel Jewell/Fernand Gravet/Fay Spain in *Goodbye, Columbus*

> J. Kostikyan, Wilton, Conn.

Barbara Rush and Mischa Auer in *Subways Are for Sleeping*

> Martin Charnin, N.Y.C.

Lee Strasberg in *Stage Coach*

> Tom Lacy, N.Y.C.
> J. F. Kearney, Bronx, N.Y.

The Man Who Wrote Dirty Books starring Irving Wallace/Irving Shulman/Irving Mansfield/Irving Stone

> Dan Greenburg, N.Y.C.

Timothy Leary in *Splendor in the Grass*

> Dr. J. W. McDonald, Cliffside Park, N.J.
> Bob and Judi DeLaurentis, Tuckahoe, N.Y.

Marlon Brando/Newton Minow in *Big Fish, Little Fish*

> Angelo R. Papa, Trenton, N.J.

High, Wide and Handsome starring Wilt Chamberlain/Jackie Gleason/Cary Grant

> Edward W. Lucas, Brooklyn, N.Y.

Separate Tables starring Henry Cabot Lodge and Nguyen Van Thieu

> Anita Witt, New City, N.Y.

Michael York and Burt Lancaster in *The War of the Roses*

> Herb Appel, N.Y.C.
> Eleanor Lurie, River Edge, N.J.

Brief Encounter with Ernest Borgnine and Ethel Merman

> Connie Wolfe, N.Y.C.
> Raymond Richard, Bayshore, N.Y.

Strom Thurmond and Richard Nixon in *Friendly Persuasion*

> David Shire, N.Y.C.

Joan Fontaine and Olivia de Havilland in *My Sister, My Love* with Warren Beatty, Shirley MacLaine

Christine Jorgensen in *I, A Woman—Part II*

> Sandy Harmon, N.Y.C.

☞ *Do You Recommend Pouilly-Fuissé?* . . .

Gentlemen:
I am a university-educated, twice-divorced, top-level executive, age thirty-four. My fiancée's parents are simple working-class people who object to our marriage, feeling we are not socially compatible. How can one convince ignorant low-income oldsters that class distinctions no longer exist? (Also do you recommend Pouilly-Fuissé or Bordeaux with a fish course?)

A. O., N.Y.C.

Above, an imaginary excerpt from *The Playboy Adviser*. Competitors were invited to submit a typical letter directed to the editor of any department in a well-known newspaper or magazine.

The New York Times Book Review
Z.B.L. writes: "Maurice B. N. Parkleigh-Dennell concluded his poem 'Carrots at Lake Saloux' with the line 'Tis full the heavy riders crunch/Withal our guests' red bounty munch.' Who are the 'guests' referred to in this line, and what were Parkleigh-Dennell's middle names?"

Bruce Feld, Bronx, N.Y.

The New York Times Book Review
For a work in progress, I would appreciate receiving letters written by Mrs. Jacqueline Kennedy Onassis (1929–?). Originals only, with greatest appreciation assured for hand-written, personal correspondence, particularly from White House years.

—CHAS. HAMILTON, N.Y.C.
James F. Graham, N.Y.C.

The New York Times Book Review
Gentlemen: Although I was pleased to find my book, *Henry James—The Opaque Crystal,* reviewed so prominently in the *Times,* I was somewhat surprised at your choice of E. Wilkinson as reviewer. As almost everyone knows, Professor Wilkinson was not only my student, but my first wife, a circumstance that in an ideal world should not have influenced her judgment, but that in this less-than-perfect one seems to have done precisely that. Far more disturbing to the scholar, however, is the fact that Professor Wilkinson's particular competence is not Henry James at all, but Edith Wharton. This may seem a small distinction to the generalists on your staff, but it is not easily dismissed by Jamesians or, indeed, by Whartonians, who tend to cherish their differences, imperceptible as they may seem to the outsider. In the expansive ranks of Modern Literature, I am convinced that it would, with a bit of effort, have been possible to find a reviewer from whom I had not recently been divorced. Your readers, some of whom are undoubtedly members of the MLA, are entitled to an explanation.

Elaine Kendall, Princeton, N.J.

Dear Dr. Franzblau: I am writing to you about my son. He is just not like the other boys. Although we are humble people (my husband is a carpenter and my son, through a mix-up in hotel reservations, was born in a barn), I have done my best to interest him in his father's business and in the daily life of our small community. However, he tends to be far too introspective and has lately developed a rather piercing look which makes me uneasy. I try to teach him proper respect for his elders and what does he do but go right off to the temple and make a lot of smart-ass remarks to the older men. He had the nerve to call *that* his father's business! To top it off, he has now gone and acquired twelve weird friends who follow him everywhere and treat him like some sort of god. None of them work and they never worry about anything. What is a mother to do?

Mary Ellen Houck, N.Y.C.

The New York Times Book Review
E.S. of New Rochelle would like to know the origin and completion of this first line of verse: "There once was a hermit named Dave . . ."

Andrew and Renee Herz, N.Y.C.

Scientific American
Sirs: Professor Zygote, in "Pagan Variation of Irish Pre-history: Two Tableaux," makes unwarranted assumptions about pagan tribal nature. Evidence from archaeological sites must lead to the conclusion that no sinodious gatherings took place prior to the introduction of the Talmud, indeed, that Ireland was devoid of piquant monotheism until that time. Although this refutes the postulations of Heimlink in "Zeitschrift Gesichtlicher Gewohnheit des Grossbritannien," insofar as Section Three is concerned, it does explain some of the hetero-geodetic errors made of late.

Steven Wangsness, Tucson, Ariz.

A.M.A. Journal
Medical News Editor: Your recent article, "Skin Conditions for Fun and Profit," included a picture titled "a rare

skin thing." It is rare indeed! It is the birthmark of the royal family of Abuvnutting. Its bearer must be our Prince, George the Missing, kidnaped at birth from the royal cottage by fun-loving gypsies from the picturesque mountains which surround our friendly valley kingdom. We would appreciate it if you could give us the address of our Prince. Speed is of the utmost importance since our summer festival starts in three weeks.

—B. ALLESCUE, CH. OF COMM., ABUVNUTTING
Dick Mendelsohn, N.Y.C.

New York Magazine
Editor: Investigation of Leonardo da Vinci's notebooks and of Richard Maltby's birth certificate demonstrates, without a doubt, that Dan Greenberg is really a crypto-anagram for Miss M. A. Madden.

DANGREENBERG
NIDSAMMDEMAS

Changing an "E" in the last syllable of a name to a "U" is an old cryptographic trick and fools no one.

—H. SARGUNT, N.Y.C.
Arthur Penn, Philadelphia, Pa.

The Wall Street Journal
Editor: Your recent article regarding the bond yield non-recurring structures in the yield curves as a ratio to abso-lute supply-demand factors of the liquidity feature within the parameter expansion of the International Monetary Fund missed the essential point. Actually, the dichoto-mous pressure manifested by the intangible hyperbolic section does in fact colineate the impalpable intersection of the 1945–1955 base period by twenty per cent. This is a point well worth considering.

Joseph H. Clinard, Jr., N.Y.C.

Jack and Jill
Editor: I enjoy your magazine very much, but shouldn't you call it "Jill and Jack"? —B. FRIEDAN, N.Y.C.
Beatrice Ballance, N.Y.C.

Humpty Dumpty
Editor: I get your magazine every month. My daddy gets his magazine every month too. I like his better because of all the mommies in it. Why don't you ever have pictures of mommies in *Humpty Dumpty*?

Sue Wallach, Roslyn Heights, N.Y.

Dear Ann Landers: A widow of sixty-seven, confined to my bed, I've found a man in his twenties who truly loves me. Monty, who gave up a steady job at a gas station to move in and care for me, is a dream, joking with me, feeding me cocoa, and making me take my medicine. My jealous children insist he's a fortune hunter, and their nagging has made me sicker. Monty tried to dissuade me from naming him my sole heir, but I've done it just to show them. Their callousness has made me so weak and hazy, I can barely finish this letter. Please tell me what to do about my ungrateful children.

Lawrence Eisenberg, N.Y.C.

The New York Times Book Review
In answer to a Mr. R.M.N. of Washington, D.C., as to the finish of the quote beginning "You can fool . . ." we believe he has in mind: "You can fool some of the people some of the time, but you can't fool us."

—VIETNAM PEACE PARADE COMM.
Allan B. Smith, N.Y.C.

Dear Dr. Franzblau: My son, a fifty-year-old college graduate, has been seeing a girl for seventeen years and is now planning to be married to her. She is not of the same faith as my son and this fact is upsetting to his father and me. We have always given him the best of everything at no small sacrifice to ourselves. Should we consent to this potentially dangerous marriage? I know he has respect for our feelings and must realize how deeply he is hurting us.

Francine Zaslow, Port Washington, N.Y.

The Daily News
Editor: May I offer my unqualified congratulations upon your recent editorial condemning the Senate rejection of the nomination of Judge Carswell. Your view is historiographically sound and unquestionably in the proud American tradition. The commie dupes and punks who continue to reject the application of law and order to hippies, homos, and hopheads should go back where they came from. I say, God bless you, sirs, in your never-ending quest for a strong, proud America. The Godless Monolith is strengthening its hold everywhere, and patriotic Americans honor your unflinching courage in standing firm for True Americanism. Keep the Faith, Baby.

—A. M. SCHLESINGER
Daniel F. Tritter, N.Y.C.

Drama Mailbag, *New York Times*
Sirs: I just cannot believe that your Mr. Barnes saw the same play I did at the Stanley Hyman Theatre. The night I was there the audience loved it! If your Mr. Barnes had even a cursory knowledge of fourteenth-century Bessarabian drama he would have recognized the fresh values imparted by this new, gifted young playwright to the Brechtian structure.

David Yarnell, N.Y.C.

The Saturday Evening Post
Subscription Dept.: This is my sixth and final letter to you. My previous correspondence resulted in no replies. I

have not been receiving my regular issues of your fine magazine for some time. I am now angry enough to take legal action. Additionally, I am sending copies of this letter to Governor Dewey, Att. Gen. Brownell, and Norman Rockwell.

Paul Noble, N.Y.C.

Dear Heloise: Here is a handy dandy little helper that we use around our house. In order to save money on paper plates, we buy the plastic-coated kind! Sure, it costs a little more to begin with, but . . .

Mrs. C. Gruenenfelder, Bellerose, N.Y.

New York Magazine
Underground Gourmet: My bender now ended/all kitchen attended/Herewith my report I submit/John's pizza was yummy/A groove for the tummy/A cool gastronomical hit/I have no contention with your honorable mention/On that we closely compare/But Goldberg's I found/though essentially round/was sensually πr^2.

Rose Sheppard, N.Y.C.

High Fidelity
Editor: Thank you for the fine review of my latest album, but your reviewer called it *Champagne Polkas*, whereas it is actually entitled *Champagne Waltzes*. *Champagne Polkas* was my last album, which he called *Champagne Tangos*, a title I used in 1968. I am enclosing a test pressing of my next album, a two-record set of *Champagne Marches and Lullabies*. Happy listening.

—LAWRENCE WELK
David Hanigan, N.Y.C.

Glamour
Beauty Editor: I am making plans to take a walking tour of Europe this summer. As I must limit my wardrobe to

what I can carry in a knapsack, would you plan about half-a-dozen formal and informal ensembles around a Saint Laurent scarf, two jersey dresses, and a pair of hiking boots?

Judith Saperstein, Millerton, N.Y.

New York Times
Travel Editor: I cannot conceive why Mr. Murray Bolshov, in his letter of June 7, should complain of the service in Paris establishments during the summer season. Last year, while our apartments in the embassy were redecorated, my wife and I had to put up at a small hotel on the Place Vendôme. We were both surprised and delighted by the ease with which our accommodations were secured, by the courteous efficiency of the management, and by the eagerness with which the staff served us. With the sole exception of tepid chocolate on a single morning, our stay was perfect.

James Fechheimer, Glen Head, N.Y.

Scientific American
Editor: Can cows tell the difference between day and night? I'm thinking of doing all my milking a few hours later to give me and the husband more sleep, but I'd hate to confuse the cows. I thought to take a lantern along to see what I was doing.   —MRS. O'LEARY, CHICAGO, ILL.

George Malko, N.Y.C.

Dear Dr. Franzblau: I am married to a wonderful man who is keeping a wonderful mistress. We have two wonderful children who have made several wonderful recoveries from drug addiction. I would tell you my problem except that you always immediately recommend visiting a therapist. But now that I have unburdened myself to you, I feel so much better. Thank you.

Michael Schreiber, Brooklyn, N.Y.

Popular Photography

Editor: How delighted I was to read your exciting review of the new Niponichi miniature dotomatic reflex action with automated paralex rotating range-finder. I agree. It does make picture-taking so much more meaningful.

Marvin Goodman, N.Y.C.

Life

Editor: As a twenty-nine-year-old mother of ten, I resent your recent articles and cover story on population control. Being well educated and happily married to a successful attorney, please be advised that I am completely contented with the present status of my hearth and home. My husband and I find your editorials on people-pollution very derogatory. In future issues we would appreciate more articles on: teen-age drug addiction, legalized abortion, psychiatric counseling for the suburban housewife.

Mrs. Christine Laspia, Rowayton, Conn.

Village Voice

Editor: As a man who is aware of the numerous forms of oppression existing in our world, I would like to thank you for printing an excellent article on Women's Liberation. These women have a legitimate grievance against our male-dominated society. I made my wife read the article twice, and I told her that as the wife of a liberal candidate for public office, she had better raise her consciousness level.

I. Redfield, Brooklyn, N.Y.

Photoplay Magazine

Queries Editor: Where do I write to Gloria Jean? Is Tricia considering a Hollywood career? How old is Lassie; is she a mother? Is Iris Adrian a natural blonde? What are Tony Bill's measurements?

Tom Morrow, N.Y.C.

☞ *Kiddy Foil*

Shed Roe   **Scionara**   **Bumbino**
Off Spring   **Kiddy Foil**   **Heir Pollution**
Junior Miss **Ova Kill**   **Teeny Bopper**

Above, some suggested commercial names for The Pill. Competitors were invited to submit brand names for real or invented products found in a drugstore.

Repeats: The Pill: No Kidding, Lower Birth, Avoid the Issue, Litter Bug, Love's Labour's Lost, Skidoo, Miss-conception. Hair Restorers: Hair Apparent, Balderdash. Deodorants: Pit Stop, Arrivederci Aroma. Miscellaneous: Antie Maim Insecticide, Drip Dry Cold Tablets, Damitol Tranquilizers.

MILHOUSE Tranquilizers

AG-NU Tongue Depressor

GAY BLADE AC/DC Electric Shaver

Charles Maguire, Chevy Chase, Md.

GENE FOWLER The Pill

ALEXANDER PUSHKIN Bargain Suppository

B'NAI B'RITH Kosher Mouthwash

Herb Sargent, N.Y.C.

ANTIRHEUM Decongestant

ANTIBELLUM Stomach Remedy

ANTISEEDANT The Pill

Jay Gubitz, N.Y.C.

COVEN TREE Witch Hazel

NO-DOGE Cyanide

BURPIE'S Flower-Scented Indigestion Tablets

Maybelle Hall, N.Y.C.

BUNKER HILL Eye Drops

Alaskan Drugstore Products:
KODIAK Camera Film

GEORGE ARMSTRONG Frozen Custard

Michael Deskey, N.Y.C.

Call Girl's Implement for Client Listing: SHTUPTIC
PENCIL

Lynn Johnson, Bryn Mawr, Pa.

JUDGE CRATER'S Vanishing Cream

CHEWSDAY Multiple Vitamins

BISMARCK'S Prussic Acid

Gladys Maguire, Chevy Chase, Md.

The Pill:
WOMB FORWENT

NIHIL OBSTET

Mary Kleve, N.Y.C.

SUNNYSIDE OOP! The Pill

Sanford Kaye, Teaneck, N.J.

Crummy Toilet Articles (div. of Wrecksall):
GO BAD DE PARIS Parfum

DRECK Shampoo

Raymond S. Kauders, N.Y.C.

The Pill:
HUMANAE VETO

ANTITOTANUS

Rev. Basil Colasito, Farmingdale, N.Y.

Bathroom Decor Accessories:
VANITIES FAIR

PRESIDENTIAL CABINETS

James Fechheimer, Glen Head, N.Y.

PROMO-SELTZER Remedy for Press Agentry

LEFT GUARD The Revolutionary Antiperspirant

Hank Levinson, N.Y.C.

ABSORBINE JUNIOR The Pill

Ed Hiestand, Westport, Conn.
Susan Cross, Indianapolis, Ind.

NIGHT CRULLERS Sleep-Inducing Wafers

Martha Everds, N.Y.C.

MICKEYMYCIN Children's Antibiotic

R. and K. White, Piermont, N.Y.

CANE AND ABLE Rheumatism Appliance

EUREKA Cheap Italian Perfume

Ruth Katz, Brooklyn, N.Y.

WHISTLE STOP Denture Adhesive

Reuben Lozner, Chevy Chase, Md.

CODEINE LONGET Cough Drops Endorsed by Andy Williams

Susan Rodin, Hollis Hills, N.Y.

SLOUGH OFF DESPOND Diet Pills

TANGENTIALLY Sunburn Lotion

V. R. Jacobs, East Orange, N.J.

SUCRET OF SANTA VITTORIA Wine-Flavored Throat Lozenges

Joel Cohen, N.Y.C.

THEY SHOOT HORSE DON'T THEY? Syringes

Jerry Orbach, N.Y.C.
Joanne Tomaselli, N.Y.C.

PASTA FA ZOO Pet Food

HETEROSOX Unisex Footgear

G. and D. Ullman, Los Angeles, Calif.

STARE CASE Men's Compact

Tap Osborn, Marion, Mass.

INFANT ASIDE The Pill

David Smilow, South Orange, N.J.

KIDDYAP The Pill

Freida Arkin, N.Y.C.

MASSAGE FROM GARCIA Liniment

Marvin Safir, N.Y.C.

KINDER GUARDIAN The Pill

Anthony M. Egan, N.Y.C.

CAPISTRANO SWALLOWS Lozenges

Gene Obert, Richmond, Va.

☞ *From Poland, with Love*

Fiddler on the Porch
Eight Lives Cat Food
From Poland, with Love
The Socks of the Fisherman
Why Junior Can't Reed

Above, some near-miss nomers. Competitors were invited to submit suggested titles, product names, slogans, or what-have-you of a similar just-off-the-mark variety.

Repeats: *George L, 1775, 6-Up. For Who the Bell Tolls,* Colonel Motors, *Bonnie and Claude, Moby Richard, Galoshes of Cherbourg,* "Give My Regards to Avenue of the Americas," and President Humphrey.

Lawrence of the United Arab Republic

Lady Chatterley's Very Good Friend

The Importance of Being Sincere

Tarzan of the Larger Primates

"Mercredi gras"

One of the Greatest Stories Ever Told

Hiroshima, Mon Ami

"In Your Lenten Bonnet"

Little Umber Sambo

Anne Kouts, N.Y.C.

"See the United States in Your Chevrolet"

"Don't Look a Gift Horse in the Eye"

Bison Bill Cody and Billy the Child

Joseph and His Siblings

The Nonameron

Man and Batman, by G. B. Shaw

Martin Israel, N.Y.C.

"One if by Land, and Two if Not"

"Don't Fire Till They Get Up Close"

"You Can Take Salem Out of the Country but not the Other Way Around"

Dan Greenburg, N.Y.C.

"Dr. Livingstone, I Suppose?"

The Green Bay Shipping Clerks

Jacqueline Kennedy Harlech

Marshall W. Karp, N.Y.C.

"Police Action and Peace"

" 'Tis Pity She's a Call Girl"

"Disadvantaged Bitos"

Uncle Tom's Low-Income Dwelling Unit

Hank Levinson, N.Y.C.

Guess Who Coming to Dinner?

> Frank Di Gennaro, N.Y.C.

The Colored Gentleman of the Narcissus

Benjamin Hur

The Businessman of Venice

> Fred E. Galbraith, Jr., Arlington, Va.

The Sun Comes Up, Too*

"We have met the enemy and they don't seem a bad sort."

> William T. Jeanes, Jackson, Miss.
> * Gary Catron, Washington, D.C.

The Alibi of Nat Turner

> Frederic M. Bassoff, Brooklyn, N.Y.

The Milk Train Doesn't Stop Here Anyhow

> Benson W. Tulloch, Sea Cliff, N.Y.

Why the West Was Won

> Richard Meredith, N.Y.C.

"A Cup of Coffee, a Sandwich, and Pie"

"There's a broken nose for every light on Broadway"

"Up, Up, and Around"

> Marta and Jerry Orbach, N.Y.C.

"To be or not to be; what should I do?"

> Phil Growick, Rego Park, N.Y.

The Senior Citizen and the Sea

> Elaine Kendall, Princeton, N.J.

"To Be Young, Gifted, and Dark"

> John Van Vleck, Long Island City, N.Y.

"Quoth the raven: 'Never again.' "

Martin Charnin, N.Y.C.

Rosencrantz and Guildenstern Are Unconscious

Ken and Joan Wurtzel, Brooklyn, N.Y.

The Matter with J. Robert Oppenheimer

R. Ingram, N.Y.C.

Wound the Piano Player

Mr. and Mrs. H. G. Miller, Chicago, Ill.

"They All Laughed at Amerigo Vespucci"

Robert D. Croog, N.Y.C.

Good Ole Gatsby

Nicholas Suder, Liverpool, N.Y.

The Agony and the Fun

Mark S. Goodman, N.Y.C.

Jacques Brel Is Alive and Well, Except for an Occasional Cold, and Living All Right—not Luxuriously, but All Right—in a Villa Near Paris.

David Heim, N.Y.C.

Nicholas and Alexander's

Leonard M. Pratt, Jr., N.Y.C.

212 288, by John O'Hara

Dave Terzenmayer, N.Y.C.

The Hairstylist of Seville

John Benitez, N.Y.C.

I Can Get It for You for Less Money than You Can Buy It Alone

Marc D. Levitt, Brooklyn, N.Y.

Le Bohème

"There Are No Atheists in Antholes"

Harry Lorayne, N.Y.C.

"Only Her Hairdresser Knows 100% Positively"

Beverly Slapin, Brooklyn, N.Y.

I Do, I Don't

Virginia McKeon, N.Y.C.

Irving Andronicus

The Pathetic Symphony

Alan Brien, London, England

"I, II, III, IV, V, VI, VII, VIII, VIIII, F, FI . . ."

Rees Behrendt, N.Y.C.

"Frankie and Johnny Were Movers"

Tom Morrow, N.Y.C.

Lincoln Center for the Performing Ants

De Pavillon

Herb Sargent, N.Y.C.

Go to the Windowmaker

Barbara F. Shor, N.Y.C.

☞ *Marvin Gardens,*
Realtor

Corporal Punishment, N.C.O.
Marvin Gardens, Realtor
Irving Trust, Banker

Above, fortuitous nomenclature. Competitors were invited to submit invented names with an apposite occupation.

Repeats: Justin Case, Insurance Broker; Paul Bearer, Funeral Director; Warren Peace, Diplomat; Billy Club and Paddy Wagon, Police; Pat Pending, Inventor; Jerry Built, Architect; Wanda Lust, Sally Forth, and Ellis Dee, Travel Agents; Polly Unsaturates, Dietitian; Upson Downes, Elevators; Chester Gigolo, Male Escort; Terry Cloth, Towel Manufacturer; Beth Israel and Molly Coddle, R.N.s; Gerry Mander, Alderman; Sy Clamate and Sal Hepatica, Pharmacists; Cliff Hanger and Erie Canal, Ghost Writers; Art Nouveau, Decorator; Grace Note and Barbara Seville, Singers; Kid Gloves, Boxer and Donny Brooks, Referee; Clair Voyant, Reader; Gerry Atrics, Antiques; Hope Chest, Debutante; Victoria Falls, Wigs; Pat Hand, Gambler; Lady Finger, Patty Cake, and Charlotte Russe, Bakers; Jimmy Locks, Second-story Man; Rock Bottom, Actor; Father Figure,

Mother Fixation, Cardinal Sin, Members of the Clergy; and strippers: Rose Tattoo, Gay Deceiver, Sybil Wrights, Rachel Prejudice, Ginger Snap, and Maxie Coat.

ANONYMOUS BOSCH, Germany's Unknown Soldier

PAULINE PRIVILEGE, Marriage Counselor

SWING LO, Chinese Charioteer

CHE BELLA, Italian Revolutionary

John H. Dorenkamp, Worcester, Mass.

BRIDGET REMAGEN, World War II Collaborator

MALCOLM TENT, Drama Critic

ALTHEA HOME, All-Male Escort Service

William Perry, N.Y.C.

SONNY LA MATINA, Wake-up Service

DOMINIC VOBISCUM, S. J.

JACQUELINE HYDE, Cosmetician

William Cole, N.Y.C.

SANTA FE, Deviate Philanthropist

Bob Monement, Westland, Mich.

SONYA PAPERMOON, Scenic designer

BERTHA VANATION, Silent Film Star*

LOIS CARMEN DENOMINATOR, Math Teacher

MARCIA DIMES, Charity Worker

NOAH VAIL, Champion of Lost Causes

Charles H. Israels, N.Y.C.
* Alan R. Greengrass, N.Y.C.

"TEX" SHELTER, Gentleman Rancher

MERCEDES BENZ, Deep-sea Diver*

REPRESENTATIVE SAMPLING, Congressman

> *Imre G. Horvath, N.Y.C.*
> ** Arnold Gray, N.Y.C.*

FAITH ANN BEGORRA, M.P., Ulster*

SIS BOOMBAW, Girls' Basketball Coach

> *Mr. and Mrs. J. W. Davis, Princeton, N.J.*
> ** Paul Zara, Chicago, Ill.*

"ARMS" MORATORIUM, Wrestler

TENNESSEE VALLEY AUTHORITY, Singer

> *Michael Lynne, N.Y.C.*

STANNOUS FLUORIDE, Shipping Magnate

> *Mrs. Myron S. Miller, N.Y.C.*

DEE MEISTERSINGER, Seamstress

ADAM BAUM, Nuclear Physicist

MORRIS MINOR, Designer of Children's Easy Chairs

> *Dan Greenburg, N.Y.C.*

BARB WIRE, Fence

T.V. SERIES, Pilot

DOLLY IN, Cinematographer

> *Thomas Klunzinger, Detroit, Mich.*

THELONIOUS ASSAULT, Mugger

EMIL NITRITE, Swinger

> *Tucker Ashworth, N.Y.C.*

JUAN TWOTHREE, Spanish Mathematician

HONDALAYO, Polynesian Motorcycle Doxy

Richard J. Richmond, Westerly, R.I.

CHARLOTTE AMALIE, Island Virgin

E. Bernstein, Brooklyn, N.Y.

MARSHA LOU PARKWAY, Urban Planner

"ARMS" AKIMBO, Japanese Wrestler

JIMMY CRACKCORN, English Folk Singer

Ted Sennett, Closter, N.J.

ELDER BERRY WINE, Minister

ALMA MATER, M.A., Ed. D.

Marcia De Fren, N.Y.C.

EMMA GRAY, Foreign Domestics

CAROLINE RICE, Southern Recipes

Elizabeth Maguire, Chevy Chase, Md.

UNICARD, Harem Watchman

Diana Bloom, N.Y.C.

DIXIE CUP, Paper Bra Designer

Hugo Flesch, Dobbs Ferry, N.Y.

MIKE FRIGHT, Prompter

Wendy Ellner, Richland, Wash.

MADGE POINT, Tennis Referee

NEAL VARLET, Chief of Protocol

Jane Iredale, N.Y.C.

DUDLEY NIGHTSHADE, Murderer

GRADY SPECTATIONS, Scion

DAHLIA DOUBLE, Racing Fan

John Bradford, N.Y.C.

AD HOC, Pawnbroker

Jerry Touger, N.Y.C.
Marcia Wagner, Bronxville, N.Y.

"GRASS" ROOTS, Folk Singer

MOSQUITO REPELLENT, Ugly Circus Midget

STELLA LUMINARI, Italian Actress

Tom Morrow, N.Y.C.

SITTING PRETTY, Indian Hairdresser

Vic Ziegel, N.Y.C.

ANDROMEDA STRAIN, Truss Maker

JOHNNIE WALKER, Male Prostitute

BABY GRAND, Go-Go Dancer

John B. Hapgood, Quogue, N.Y.

BELLE WETHER, Fashion Editor

Carol Zaiser, N.Y.C.

ABBY PLAYER, Irish Actress

MOE PARKS, Sausage Stuffer

VICTOR SPOILS, War Surplus

ROGER OVER, Communications Expert

Hank Levinson, N.Y.C.

LES HALLES, Butcher

Lowell Bonfeld, Bronx, N.Y.

DUTCH TREAT, Cheap Gangster

> *Shelly Roberts, Chicago, Ill.*

REV. UP, Faith Healer

> *Florine McCain, N.Y.C.*

PRECIOUS STONE, Devotee of Father Divine

> *Sylvia Marx, Mamaroneck, N.Y.*

FOSTER PARENTS, Child Star

> *Jerry Moore, N.Y.C.*

ANGEL HAIR, Puerto Rican Sissy

> *Anderson Hess, N.Y.C.*

CHRISTOPHER ACTOR, Plumber

MAL ADROIT, Juggler

> *Robert Grand, N.Y.C.*

AL FRESCO, House Painter

> *Msgr. A.V. McLees, St. Albans, N.Y.*

SAUL MORGENBESSER, Procrastinator

GEORGE MONAVIS, News Commentator

> *S.O. Goran, N.Y.C.*

"SUI" GENERIS, Hog Caller Extraordinary

> *Cleo Brough, Irvington, N.Y.*

CARA NOME, Eskimo

RABBIT WARREN, Female Impersonator

> *Arthur Penn, Philadelphia, Pa.*

BUDDY SYSTEM, Camp Counselor

"FATTY" DEPOSIT, Banker

LE GRAND PALAIS, Exhibitionist

> *R. Ross, Ardmore, Pa.*

MASTER CHARGE, Son of Brig. Gen. N.O. Charge, H.M.A.S., O.B.E.

> *B. Andrew Hoffman, N.Y.C.*

REX HUNTER, Genealogist for Royalty

> *Pat Matsumoto, Chicago, Ill.*

GLORIA MUNDI, Exotic Dancer*

AGNES DAY, Zealot

> *Judith and Nelson Dunford, N.Y.C.*
> **Tom Hunter, N.Y.C.*

CHRISTOPHER STREET, Longshoreman

JANE STREET, His Wife

GAY STREET, Their Fey Son

HORATIO STREET, Their Pretentious Daughter

PRINCE STREET, His Dog

> *Richard Fithian, N.Y.C.*

SYDNEY AUSTRALIA, Kangaroo Rancher

> *Leslie Pam Harmon, N.Y.C.*
> *Joseph T. Jordan, Montclair, N.J.*

PENNY DREADFUL, Mystery Writer

> *Ronald N. Foster, Jr., N.Y.C.*

SONNY AND WARMER, Singers

> *Mrs. Randi Jospe, N.Y.C.*

HY DUDGEON, Volatile Television Director

FROGS LEGS PROVENÇAL, French Gangster

> *Robert Bochroch, N.Y.C.*

BLANCHE CARTE, Credit Adviser

> *Caterine Quill, N.Y.C.*

CANTOR BARRY BELLS, Lead Singer, Temple Emanu-El
Bill Green, N.Y.C.

BESSIE MAE MUCHO, Spanish Folk Singer
David Scoggins, N.Y.C.

SIKH BEY, Potentate

CHASE MANHATTAN, Temperance Crusader
Jay Wolf, N.Y.C.

PORT AUTHORITY, Winetasters
Elizabeth Kiernan, Larchmont, N.Y.

BARON WASTE, Land Developer
Sanford Fisher, Silver Spring, Md.

OLIVE BRANCH, Pacifist

ROSA CRUCEAN, Fortuneteller
J. C. Stanton, N.Y.C.

REV. IOLI, Vatican Cook
Patricia Newman, Brooklyn, N.Y.

PETER RAMSBOTTOM, Subway Amorist
Allen Glasser, Brooklyn, N.Y.

AUGUST DEMEANOR, Senator
Christopher Friedrichs, Princeton, N.J.

"POP" CORN, Retired Vaudevillian

ST. REGIS, Patron of Hotels
Jane Herman, N.Y.C.

BEA PREPARED, Girl Scout
Joshua Ross, D.D.S., Rockville Center, N.Y.

MATT BURNS, Wrestler

King C. Morgan, Washington, D.C.

CARMEN COLD, Epidemiologist

Miles Klein, Belle Harbor, N.Y.

SARAH N. DIPITY, Gift Specialist

Bill Jacobs, Detroit, Mich.

STUD POKER, Gigolo

WASHINGTON, D.C., Gynecologist

Ted Mingo, N.Y.C.

SEÑOR HA, Transvestite

Norma and Larry Zippin, Briarwood, N.Y.

D. AGONY & D. ECSTASY, Ceiling Painters

Richard Rosenberg, N.Y.C.

LUCINDA JOINTS, Contortionist

Pfc. Richard F. Davis, Staten Island, N.Y.

HELEN HIGHWATER, Woman Marine

Robert Luchs, Wheaton, Ill.
Dr. Robert Lowrance, N.Y.C.

PROCTOR SILEX, Associate Professor

Howard Weiss, Cliffside Park, N.J.

ELLEN M. KING, Cigarette Girl

Frank Zaza, Arlington, Va.

HAROLD TRIBUNE, Has-been

Pat Hamilton, N.Y.C.

LES MISÉRABLES, Psychiatrist

Barbara Metsky, Washington, D.C.

TAMARA DEWORLD, Espionage Agent

Jane Wharton, Seattle, Wash.

LES DANCE, Orchestra Leader

Marlene March, N.Y.C.

"CHICAGO" BAER, Linebacker

Phil Kukoff, N.Y.C.

BESS SELLER, Novelist

Monty Morgan, N.Y.C.

HON. MENTION, Judge

TEMPLE ORANGE, Buddhist Monk

Dave Willis, N.Y.C.

MONTGOMERY WARD, Rich Orphan

CROSS AND BROWN, Militants

Edward M. Roberts, Glen Head, N.Y.

☞ "A Bird in Hand Is Worth Two in the Bus"

"Look upon the rainbow and braise him who made it"

"A bird in hand is worth two in the bus"

Above, misprints due to the substitution or omission of a single letter. Competitors were invited to submit similarly altered titles, quotes, aphorisms, and the like.

Repeats: "There's No Place Like Nome," "Wish You Were Her," "Up, Up, and Awry," *Love's Labours Cost,* "I've Got You under My Ski," "A Rose is a Rose is a Ruse," "Wouldn't You Really Rather Have a Buck?," "I've Come to Bury Caesar, Not to Raise Him," *All's Well that Ends Wel,* and *A Comedy of Errers.*

"Lizzie Borden took an ale
And gave her mother forty whacks."

"All the world is queer save thee and me, and even thou art a little queen."

R. L. Bohn, Los Angeles, Calif.

The Playwrights' Company Resents Kim Stanley in *The Traveling Lady*

> *Warren Lyons, N.Y.C.*

"Black as the pit from pole to pole,
I thank whatever God may be
For my unconquerable soup."

> *Judith Klein, Belle Harbor, N.Y.*

"A Plaque on Both Your Houses"

> *R. Ralston Hill, N.Y.C.*

SMALL APARTMENT FOR RUNT

> *Fred Needhammer, Bloomingdale, N.J.*

"VIPs That Touch Liquor Shall Never Touch Mine"

> *Louis Doyle, N.Y.C.*

Rosenkrantz and Guildenstern are Deaf

> *Roderick Cook, N.Y.C.*

"There's a Somebody I'm Lunging to See"

You Know I Can't Heal You When the Water's Running

> *Karen Albamonti, N.Y.C.*

DON'T FEEL THE ANIMALS

> *B. A. Scheiner, Brooklyn, N.Y.*

"Here in My Army You're Adorable"

> *Arnold Cover, Sarasota, Fla.*

"Dog creeps in on little cat feet"

> *Dale McAdoo, N.Y.C.*

"Ruth is stranger than fiction."

> *Edward W. Powell, Jr., N.Y.C.*

"To be or not to be. What is the question?"

Paula Roizman, N.Y.C.
Susan Aronson, N.Y.C.

"And God said, Let there be light: and there was night."

Ron Wren, San Rafael, Calif.

"God help those who help themselves."

Paul Weiss, Washington, D.C.

"Little Miss Muffet sat on a tuffet, eating her curds—and why?"

D. Roger A. Kinsey, Fort Washington, N.Y.

"Something's rotten in Denmurk"

Marshall W. Karp, N.Y.C.

Bunny Lake Is Messing

Kurt K. Kroll, North Hollywood, Calif.

"What is so rare as a May in June?" *

"A fool and his Monet are soon parted."

Veronika Soul, Baltimore, Md.
*Gail Levenstein, N.Y.C.

"Do unto otters as you would have them do unto you."

Margot Best, N.Y.C.
Christine Jordan, N.Y.C.

"Each capsule contains more than 600 Tiny Tim pills"

Diane Davis, Huntington, N.Y.

"I Could Have Danced All Right"

Fr. Cronan Kelly, O.F.M., N.Y.C.
Richard Lavsky, N.Y.C.

"There was an old woman who jived in a shoe"

Lou Linder, N.Y.C.

"Good night, David." "Good night, Che."

> Beth Morganstern, N.Y.C.

Toe Shoes of the Fisherman

> Gary Belkin, N.Y.C.

Carson McCullers and Muriel Spark on banking and cosmetics: *The Ballad of the Sad Safe. The Primp of Miss Jean Brodie.*

> Joanna Steichen, N.Y.C.

"See the UJA in your Chevrolet"

> Susan Zamichow, N.Y.C.

"Love Me or Lease Me"*

The Flying Nut

> F. W. Rhines, New Canaan, Conn.
> Mrs. David A. Mortman, N.Y.C.
> *Alvin Goldstein, N.Y.C.

"A rabbi's foot brings good luck."

> Theodore H. Spaeth, N.Y.C.
> Tom Morrow, N.Y.C.

"The folks who live on the Pill"

> A. T. Hannett, N.Y.C.

"Arthur Murray Taught Me Dancing in a Hury"

> R. W. England, Kingston, R.I.

". . . and the Cabots talk only to Cod."

> Martha Fornatale, Park Ridge, N.J.

"I hate to see a grown man dry"

> Mary Morris, Brooklyn, N.Y.

Museum of Modern Arp

> Mrs. Peter Densen, N.Y.C.

Jacques Brel Is Alive and Well and Living in Parts

"Monterey Pot"

> *Matthew Golden, Brooklyn, N.Y.*

"The Greatest Story Ever Sold"

> *Elizabeth Ehrlich, Providence, R.I.*

"On the Food Ship Lollypop"

> *Karen Lampert, Roslyn, N.Y.*

There's nothing new under the UN

"Laughter on Tenth Avenue"

> *Anita Witt, New City, N.Y.*

The Unsinkable Molly Drown

> *Shelley Newell, Flushing, N.Y.*
> *Joel W. Darrow, Bronx, N.Y.*

"Don't court your chickens before they hatch"

> *L. Sandek, Nyack, N.Y.*

"We have nothing to wear but fear itself."

> *Mr. and Mrs. Benjamin Schonzeit, N.Y.C.*

The Russians Are Coming! The Russians Are Coping!

> *Selma LeVan, West Reading, Pa.*

Welfare Department, Pity of New York

> *Linda Wittman, Hackensack, N.J.*

"The Neatness of You"

> *Ina Brody, N.Y.C.*

"Mary had a little limb . . ."

> *Xerxes Mifravinoid, Malverne, N.Y.*

☞ *The Thing About This Lamb Was . . .*

The thing about this lamb was, everywhere old Mary would go, there would be this lamb and all with wool, white, all over it. They were some pair. Her and this goddam dwarfy lamb. She kills me, Old Mary.

Above, a nursery rhyme by J. D. Salinger. Competitors were invited to submit a nursery rhyme as written in the style of the Bible, Ogden Nash, Shakespeare, Hemingway, or Philip Roth.

LITTLE MISS MUFFET

Little Miss Muffet, partaking of an alfresco, skim-milk snack for elevenses,
Suddenly caught sight of a spider and ran screaming away, with many "Sakes alives!" and "Good Heavenses!"
Pointing a moral so contemporary as to be unhackneyed:
Low-calorie dairy products may not give you sufficient energy to withstand the appearance of any fly, slug, beetle or arachnid. —NASH

Roderick Cook, N.Y.C.

JACK SPRAT

Sprat tasted it. It was good, the way it tasted once. He could not remember when. Good lean meat. The old woman, she couldn't eat it. He watched as she tore at the fat with her fingers. Even then it did not still the cold hunger. They licked the platter. Old woman, he thought when they had finished, we have come a long way together. His wound ached.   —HEMINGWAY

Arnold Rosenfeld, Royal Oak, Mich.

OLD MOTHER HUBBARD

Old Mother Hubbard went to the cupboard to get her poor dog a bone. Does M.H. care the poor disgusting dog is already overweight? Does she care he has the runs from too much chicken soup? Does she care that he hates bones? No. Eat, Fido. Eat and be happy. Eat and make puppies. And her cupboard isn't bare. Who is she trying to kid?   —ROTH

Diane Gersten, Derby, Conn.

QUOTATION FROM THE BIBLE

"Thou art Peter and from this garden thou shalt pick pecks of pickled peppers."   —NEW TESTAMENT

Brenda C. Wehle, Washington, D.C.

JACK AND JILL

They lay on the pine-needle floor at the foot of the hill.

"The tumbling was fine," Jill said. "Was it good for you, Jack?"

"No," he said. "Let's not talk about the falling."

She felt of his crown. But it was no good.

"Oh, Jack," she said, "we could have had such a damned good time fetching together."

"Yes," he said. "Isn't it pretty to think so?"

—HEMINGWAY

William F. Gavin, Arlington, Va.

LITTLE JACK HORNER

Listen, doctor, wouldn't you be in trouble if your first memory, practically, had to do with a Christmas pie? A

Christmas pie! Get the significance? A Christmas pie and my mother.

Sure, my mother loved me, but yet I sat in that corner eating that pie.

"What are you doing, Jack? Yonkel, answer your mother!"

How could I tell her? She would've made a tsimmis of my Christmas pie. She would've hovered like the angel of death, but she wouldn't have passed over. Believe me!

So what did I do? Oy, it hurts me to think of it. I stuck in my thumb. That's right, I don't blame you for looking away. My *thumb!* And I pulled out a plum. Not a prune like any good Jewish boy, but a plum. Then, despite my unnatural use of that thumb on that plum, I said: "Oh, what a good boy am I!"

And my momma believed me. Doctor, except for that liver episode that's the worst thing I ever did. Not eating the Christmas pie. Not lying to my mother. No, don't you see? I used my *thumb* to eat a *plum!* Is it any wonder I've been a closet thumb sucker ever since? Oy, the shame. Oy, the hiding and deception. Oy, my thumb!   —ROTH

Irma E. Reichert, N.Y.C.

HEY DIDDLE DIDDLE

This night, Horatio, is but the daylight sick
When babes are wheedled into bed with nightmare tales
Of a monstrous hey diddle;
Of cats and fiddles, and cows leaping moons;
Of laughing dogs and dishes hie'd off with spoons.
For my own part, it is Greek to me.   —SHAKESPEARE

Charles M. Maguire, Chevy Chase, Md.

MARY MARY QUITE CONTRARY

He found Mary beautiful but difficult.

"What's in your garden?" he said.

"Silver Bells, Cockle Shells, things like that," she said.

Later they had lunch.   —HEMINGWAY

Marcia De Fren, N.Y.C.

HUMPTY DUMPTY

While you'd think that an egg would be gregarious
Humpty, an ovular chap, sought positions lonely and precarious
Despite all efforts regal
And legal
Once he went splat. That
Was that.

—NASH
David L. Underhill, Westhampton Beach, N.Y.

LITTLE MISS MUFFET

O! that these too too solid curds would melt
And thaw a whey. For hark!
What many-membered fiend
Creeps in this petty place
And fixes with arachnoid guile his sights
Where I do sit. I needs must slough it
And my quietus meet with a bare tuffet.

—SHAKESPEARE
Diane Davis, Huntington, N.Y.

PEASE PORRIDGE HOT

I wouldn't encorridge
Eating pease porridge.

—NASH
Mrs. Edward W. Powell, Jr., N.Y.C.

LITTLE JACK HORNER

I remember one Christmas. Naturally we didn't celebrate Christmas. God forbid. We had Chanukah. It was eight days long, which to my mother meant it was at least eight times better than any *goyische* holiday.

Anyway, I remember this one Christmas. The Horners next door weren't Jewish and I went over there on some phony "gotta-borrow-a-book" pretext so I could sneak a look at the forbidden tree.

Well, when I got there, Jack Horner—his real name was John, Jr., but everybody called him Jack—was sit-

ting in one corner of the dining room with a pie on his
lap. Not just a piece of pie. A whole goddam pie!

"It's Christmas pie," Mrs. Horner tells me, apparently
more disturbed about her Jewish neighbor's ignorance
than her own son's lousy table manners.

Anyway, I'm standing there trying not to gape, when
this kid, John Horner, Jr., sticks his thumb in the pie,
comes up with some kind of goddam prune on the end of
it, looks at me, and he says, "What a good boy am I."

"What a good boy am I!" Children are starving in Europe (or so I was led to believe) and this kid is pulling
prunes out of pies with his thumb and giving me lines out
of left field like "What a good boy am I."

For a while, I thought maybe it was some sort of religious thing. Maybe he meant "What a good goy am I." I
don't know.

It doesn't make any difference. The poor bastard was
killed in Korea a week before he was supposed to get his
discharge.

Even my mother cried.   —ROTH
         Marshall Karp, N.Y.C.

OLD KING COLE
King Cole, in hoary wisdom's coronet,
Prescribed th' elixir crowning all his zest:
A pipe for relaxation, bowl to whet
His thirst, a viol trio for the rest.   —SHAKESPEARE
       Arnold Cover, Sarasota, Fla.

FOR WHOM THE HORN BLOWS
The gypsy woman spat into the dust of the floor of the
barn and said for the hundredth time the name of the
shepherd boy whose job it had been to blow the horn
which was to have been the signal, their signal the signal
for which they had been waiting and waiting and which
was now long overdue, a bad omen, a very bad omen

indeed, although the gypsy woman had decided to pretend otherwise.

"*Qué va,* but I do not like it," the old man said. "I do not like it at all. The sheep is in the meadow, the cow is in the corn, and still he does not blow his horn. I obscenity on his not blowing his stinking horn."

"I obscenity in the milk of thy obscenity." The gypsy woman said: "Do not worry, old one, he will blow it."

"Where is the boy who looks after the sheep?" the old man said. "*Qué va*—I think that he is under the haystack, fast asleep." "It is a stinking mess," the old man said. "That our entire mission, and indeed, our very lives should have to depend on a worthless milk-sucker of a shepherd, with the worthless milk-sucking name of Little Boy Blue is entirely a stinking mess."

The old man spat into the dust of the floor of the barn and the gypsy woman spat into the dust of the floor of the barn and they continued to wait for the blowing of the horn which they knew would never come.

—HEMINGWAY
Dan Greenburg, N.Y.C.

☞ *A Subject Appealing and Fit . . .*

A subject appealing and fit
For Limericks laden with wit
Is: "Life in Fun City."
Invent one such ditty,
Competitors, please, and submit.

Competitors were invited to compose limericks lamenting the hazards of city living.

The city's a gem; why ignore it?
Acclaim it, enjoy it, explore it.
Take a walk, day or dark,
Any street, any park—
I, Sacher-Masoch, adore it!

Ira Levin, N.Y.C.

Our New York policemen wear dresses,
To draw lonely rapists' caresses.
But rapists can spot 'em,
So why have we got 'em?
Policemen enjoy it, my guess is.

Jack Labow, N.Y.C.

In dreams, there's a guy in pursuit. He
Is driving a cab, calls me "cutie,"
He begs and he pleads,
Says I fill all his needs,
But I sneer and reply, "I'm off duty."

Alice M. Yohalem, N.Y.C.

If ever New York thinks it's licked it,
Recall that last Christmas depicted
Near Powell's shining steeple
A few Harlem people,
Ill-clad and alone—and evicted.

Lloyd M. Perell, N.Y.C.

When that great 5-cent ride I compare
With today's 30-center, I swear,
Let a token resistance
Enforce our insistence
To bring back the old laissez fare!

Joel Cohen, N.Y.C.

A lady set out for the Met,
Bejeweled and beaded with jet,
It was then her bad luck
That the lift became stuck,
Which was one Otis more to regret.

Mrs. Edward W. Powell, Jr., N.Y.C.

St. Patrick, Columbus, Pulaski,
Parades on their days are fiasci,
Trying to drive
Across Avenue Five
Is a feat that requires a passkey.

Herb Sargent, N.Y.C.

It's not horns honking all through my dinner,
Nor the fact that my hair's getting thinner

That makes me cry.
But hard as I try,
Herb Sargent is always the winner.

Irene DeBlasio, N.Y.C.

The street drill said rack-a-tack-tack,
The subway went rackety-clack,
"What'd you say?" said the teller.
"Please speak louder, feller!"
"Never mind," said the thief, "I'll come back."

Mary E. Houck, N.Y.C.

Imagine what's down in the sewer,
A Spauldeen, a thumbtack, a skewer,
A red hat, fried rice,
A *Newsweek,* some mice,
And a catfish that's bigger than you are.

A. Rosenberg, N.Y.C.
B. Altenhein, N.Y.C.

On a cold day, a mod lass, Miss Segal,
In her Bloomingdale's maxicoat regal,
Inadvertently swept,
And on hem-line she kept
The effects of a boxer and beagle.

E. A. Lang, N.Y.C.

New York atmosphere's funnily smoking
With pollution rib-tickling and poking;
It's really a gas,
A howling morass,
Except I'm in no mood for choking.

Jack Paul, Brooklyn, N.Y.

A New Yorker, displeased with the things
That his life in the city now brings
Is leaving quite soon

For a trip to the moon.
We could all use this Gothamer's wings.

Michael Brimm, Cambridge, Mass.

After searching since last January,
I've found an apartment! How merry!
Just how did I get it?
Well, silly, I read it
In yesterday's obituary.

Mrs. Bunny Daniels, Hewlett, N.Y.

A New Yorker who's moved to D.C.,
I find I now breathe easily.
Why it's no surprise is
Because hot air rises,
And government's our main industry.

Anita Siner, Washington, D.C.

New Yorkers are really unsinkable.
The water they drink isn't drinkable,
There's garbage and grime,
Pollution and crime.
Live anywhere else? It's unthinkable.

Emily Barnhart, Pittsburgh, Pa.

There once was a lass from Fun City,
Who found more than the nitty was gritty.
As she climbed, in her maxi,
To enter a taxi,
The door turned it into a midi!

Helaine Lesnick, Scarsdale, N.Y.

You may not know whether you oughter
Breathe the air, eat the food, or drink water,
But you can be sure

That the plays are impure,
So don't take your mother or daughter.

Virginia B. Feine, Hartford, Conn.

That space has a hydrant, so pass it!
(Don't feel like a woebegone basset!)
You reach Lincoln Center:
"Garage Full! Don't Enter!
Available Room in Manhasset."

James Fechheimer, Glen Head, N.Y.

The late news was not good on Sunday;
"Tomorrow the subways won't run." They
Called a chanteuse
And gave her the news,
"Sick transit, Gloria, Monday!"

John Cunha, Islip, N.Y.

We've pollution, corruption, and smogs,
Plus the garbage and traffic that clogs,
But the prize for the worst
(If we don't go there first),
Must certainly go to the dogs.

Patricia Remer, Miami, Fla.

With the girls of New York I see red,
When by copycat fashions they're led.
If there's one thing that's worse
Than her scarf on her purse,
It's her glasses on top of her head.

Michael Deskey, N.Y.C.

The halls of my building are blighted,
The landlord has rarely been sighted,
My woe is complete,

Though my seven-room suite
For one-twenty is not to be slighted.

Joe Masteroff, N.Y.C.

Said the lady upstairs who sublets,
"What with smokestacks and diesels and jets,
It doesn't seem fair
Just to get some clean air
I've got filters on my cigarettes."

Felix Kulka, San Francisco, Calif.

The charms of New York are exquisite,
But to get in and out isn't—is it?
Its faults I forgive,
It's a great place to live,
But a helluva nuisance to visit.

Edith Blanchard, Portland, Conn.

It's five and you've had a tough day,
Now for dinner, relax at a play.
Flag a cab, see him swerve. Is
He ready for service?
Of course! If you're going his way!

Allen L. Taylor, N.Y.C.

On a city street corner: "Absurd,"
Shouts one man, "the new rumor I've heard
That this din that we hear,
Could do harm to the ear."
Says the other, "I can't hear a word."

Katherine Lewis, Bemidji, Minn.

Your throat oft implores you to drench it,
But a thirst at a show? Try to bench it.
The vari-ade there

Is petite and so *chère,*
Costs a dollah a swallah to quench it.

Jeni Caplan, N.Y.C.

There's dirt on the streets, to be sure.
And the air that we breathe is impure,
So why are we vexed
At our films grossly sexed,
And the paper-bound lecherature?

Milton J. Pensak, N.Y.C.

"The people!" cried John the all-knowing,
"A mandate for action bestowing,
Could one want for more?"
Then he peeked out the door
And cautiously asked, "Is it snowing?"

Christine Guinta, Bridgeport, Conn.

There was an express train at eight,
I missed it and now I'll be late.
I could take the local,
But just to be vocal,
I'll swear and complain and I'll wait.

Evan Cooper, Brooklyn, N.Y.

The ferry is always on time,
Fewer junkies, more trees, and less grime.
Confrontation is rare,
John J. Marchi lives there,
You can get there and back for a dime.

Richard Enquist, Brooklyn, N.Y.

Sing "Hi" for the dashing commuter,
One thing he's not getting is muter,
"For the riders at large,
Cleopattera's barge,
Would be quicker and slicker and cuter."

Kenneth Agnew, Jr., N.Y.C.

New York has an air that's unique.
It isn't a smell—it's a reek,
An odor senescent,
Foul, noxious, putrescent,
But I miss it when gone for a week.

Michael Sage, N.Y.C.

After work when I'm tired and tense,
I walk underground where it's dense.
I can't breathe in that air,
And it just isn't fair,
That for this I am charged thirty cents!

Laurie Grad, N.Y.C.

"Those municipal snowplows!" you blurb,
"Their work after storms is superb!"
Then you reach a cleared street
And sink both your feet
Where Alps rise on Alps at the curb.

Mary Catherine O'Connor, Convent, N.J.

When your mail brings you letters from hicks,
Delighted to get in their licks,
By limericks witty
Against our fair city,
Remember they come from the sticks!

Msgr. A.V. McLees, St. Albans, N.Y.

☞ *Lady Macbeth Hand Laundry*

Lady Macbeth Hand Laundry
Lot's Wife, Spices and Condiments
Krakatoa Plate Glass and Mirror Company

Above, excerpts from an unusual classified directory. Competitors were invited to submit listings associated with famous persons, places, or events.

Repeats: Mme. Defarge Knitwear, Lewis Hershey Greeting Cards, M. Antoinette Pastries, Christiaan Barnard Pumps, Neil Armstrong Cheeses, KKK Linens, Procrustes Adjustments, Penelope Reweaving, Raquel Welch Body Shop, Oedipus Optometrists, LBJ Aviary, Moses Tours, Hoover Hearing Aids, Khrushchev Shoe Repair, Delilah Barbers, and Samson Wrecking.

GAZA OPTOMETRISTS

GILEAD SALVE AND OINTMENTS, INC.

BOSWORTH FIELD HOSTLERS
AND LIVERY STABLE

Ira S. Mothner, N.Y.C.

TORQUEMADA & ASSOCIATES
Public Opinion Research

CHATTERLEY & MELLORS
Outdoor Parties

DANTE ALIGHIERI
Retirement Communities
Henry W. Levinson, N.Y.C.

JUDAS ISCARIOT CUSTOM FRAMING

AMANDA "KITTY" BLAKE SAFETY
DEVICES
Be Careful Matts

DIONNE-FISCHER REPRODUCTION-
DUPLICATING EQUIPMENT
Carol Drew, Palisades Park, N.J.

SIMEON STYLITES STATIONERY

LEANDER HERO SANDWICHES
Joe William Earnest, Colorado City, Texas

POLLY ADLER AND BENJAMIN SPOCK
Pick-Ups & Deliveries
William L. Tynan, N.Y.C.

W. C. FIELDS DAY NURSERY*

TEXAS MINIATURES
Roderick Cook, N.Y.C.
* *P. Cenci, Baltimore, Md.*

STELLA KOWALSKI
Specialist in Animal Husbandry
Sher Joseph, Washington, D.C.

OSCAR WILDE
Gentleman's Gentleman
Ronald K. Marshall, Kansas City, Mo.

JOHN ALDEN
Suits Pressed
Gerald Kilcullen, Jamaica, N.Y.

BOTTICELLI OYSTER BAR
Anne Mahony, N.Y.C.

I. WALTON CAT FOOD
Trudi Lanz, Port Chester, N.Y.

IAGO SCARFS
Barry Deutsch, Wyncote, Pa.

KAMA SUTRA: Positions Wanted
J. H. Crawford, N.Y.C.

DREW PEARSON
Roomers by Day or Week
Patricia Koenigsberg, N.Y.C.

HENRIK IBSEN
Ghost Writer
J. F. Daly, Passaic, N.J.

BASTILLE STORM DOORS AND WINDOWS
Rudy Ruderman, Scarsdale, N.Y.

THANKLESS CHILD BLADE CO.
A Lear Industry
Michael Glenn-Smith, N.Y.C.

LIZABETH SCOTT
Lectrician
Pearl Belkin, N.Y.C.

PLATO BONDED ESCORT SERVICE
William E. Pensyl, Sarasota, Fla.

POINT O' WOODS HERRING AND CHITLINS

STONEHENGE CALENDAR CO.
Martin Israel, N.Y.C.

BUENOS AIRES BUREAU
OF MISSING PERSONS
Eleanor Sullivan, N.Y.C.

JACK THE RIPPER
Piece Work
AVERELL HARRIMAN
Peace Work
JOLLY GREEN GIANT
Peas Work
Jack O'Brien, Forest Hills, N.Y.

TWELVE DISCIPLES FISH MARKET
Norman Storer, White Plains, N.Y.

O. & W. WRIGHT
Bird Imitations
Judd Woldin, South Orange, N.J.

MINOTAUR PSYCHOLOGICAL TESTING
David Traktman, N.Y.C.

PROFESSOR HIGGINS
Stereo-typing
Diane Brumbaugh, Hatboro, Pa.

TIRESIAS, UNISEX BOUTIQUE

FERDINAND FINE GLASS AND CHINA
Samuel Rolston, N.Y.C.

CHICKEN LITTLE NEWS SERVICE
William Carr, Washington, D.C.

HELEN GURLEY BROWN
Catered Affairs

Liz Smith, N.Y.C.

SALEM, MASS., ARTS AND CRAFTS
Hugh Manning, Brooklyn, N.Y.

DORIAN GRAY
Paintings Restored

MEDUSA HEADSTONES
Hal Stein, Somerset, N.J.

ORPHEUS REAR VIEW MIRRORS

WHITE HOUSE LINEN AND
LAUNDRY SERVICE,
Mary Gallagher, Prop.
Charles Maguire, Chevy Chase, Md.

PYGMALION KINETIC SCULPTURES
Michael Deskey, N.Y.C.

JOHN WAYNE'S SCHOOL A ELACUTION
Gloria Ullman, Los Angeles, Calif.

PALEY: PARK—DAY AND NIGHT
Joe Masteroff, N.Y.C.

WM. SHAKESPEARE AND PENELOPE ASHE
Purveyors of Bacon & Tripe
Dorothy Abrams, N.Y.C.

E. E. CUMMINGS
Typewriter Repair
Judith Page, N.Y.C.

CARRIE NATION BOTTLE STOPPERS LTD.

BIG BAD WOLF BLOWER SYSTEMS
Tom Morrow, N.Y.C.

BERIA, BULGANIN, MALENKOV, AND
KHRUSHCHEV OFFICE TEMPORARIES
Rees Behrendt, N.Y.C.

JOYCE KILMER
Lumber

Karl Levett, N.Y.C.

MACHIAVELLI & ASSOCS.
Executive Recruitment

Cyril C. Penn, N.Y.C.

R. NIXON
Eighteenth-Century
Cabinetry

C. Mack, N.Y.C.

BUDA PEST EXTERMINATORS
Mrs. Reginald Oliver, N.Y.C.

JONAH'S MOBILE HOMES

CHAS. GOREN
Contractor

Harvey Hoffman, Houston, Texas

CASPAR, MELCHIOR, AND BALTHASAR: GIFTS
"We Deliver"

Ralston Hill, N.Y.C.

ARMAGEDDON SURPLUS STORES
Allan Forsyth, N.Y.C.

SCARLETT O'HARA
Fortunes Told

Kate Holliday, Los Angeles, Calif.

ABRAHAM AND SARAH
Antique Reproductions

Clarice Golden, N.Y.C.

EMILE ZOLA
Jacuzzi Whirlpool Baths

James H. Burke, N.Y.C.

LITTLE BO PEEP
Stockbroker

Charles Poret, N.Y.C.

SONNY TUFTS DETECTIVE AGENCY
Missing Persons

James Kirkwood, East Hampton, N.Y.

JOE PENNER POULTRY

Evelyn Kaye, Miami Beach, Fla.

GOLDWATER'S DEPARTMENT STORE
Liberal Discounts

William S. Weiss, Brooklyn, N.Y.

GULLIVER: SUITS, COATS, DRESSES
Sizes 1 to 397

George Mueller, Los Angeles, Calif.

ISHMAEL ANSWERING SERVICE

Gon Firpo, N.Y.C.

WALT WHITMAN
Lawn Care

Marion Neve, Denver, Colo.

SALVADOR DALI
Watch Repair

Fred Cline, N.Y.C.
C. and J. Probst, Nashville, Tenn.

THE WEARY TRAVELER ROADSIDE PUB
(formerly St. Christopher's Inn)

Spyros Root, N.Y.C.

ARMSTRONG, ALDRIN, AND COLLINS
Long Distance Movers

Jean M. Giesberg, Houston, Texas

HARRY KRISHNA
Oriental Specialties

Merry Silver, N.Y.C.

BOBBY FISHER
Pawnbroker

Otto J. Steith, Jr., Yonkers, N.Y.
H. E. Godett, Kew Gardens, N.Y.

RICHARD DALEY
Pork Products

Thomas Grubisich, Reston, Va.

RODERICK USHER
Demolition

W. A. Gumberts, Evansville, Ind.
John J. Schiano, Brooklyn, N.Y.

PENTAGON BRASS WORKS
Lew Powell, Greenville, Miss.

PRINCE HAMLET
Theatre Parties

Mrs. Alex Mittelman, San Rafael, Calif.

ELIHU YALE, MERRILL LYNCH, GARY COOPER
Locks, Stocks, Barrels

Sheldon Biber, Union City, N.J.

THE SETTING SUN HORSE FARM
H.R.H. Eliz. II, Prop.

Nadja Root, N.Y.C.

ALEXANDER THE GREAT
Real Estate

Mrs. Leo Petit, Jr., Tunis, Tunisia

☞ *"Plink! Plonk!"*

**Plink! Plonk! Raindrops begin
Christopher Robin is soaked to the skin**

She stood trembling before him, revealed in
her lush, overripe willingness. He ached for
her. "Magda," he managed, "wouldn't you
really rather have a Buick?"

Above, a weather report by A. A. Milne, a commercial by Harold Robbins. Competitors were
invited to submit, in the style of a well-known
writer, a recipe, weather report, Dear John letter, joke, commercial, household hint, sermon,
campaign speech, prescription, spy message,
subscription renewal form, marriage proposal,
or letter of resignation.

Subscription Renewal
Dear Subscriber:
I am sitting at night in a deserted office in the subscription department, and it is January, and it is cold. I cannot
seem to keep warm, even with the frayed gray carpet
from the editor's office draped around my shoulders.

Sitting here at my desk in the empty room, I suddenly
begin to cry. My husband calls on the night line and tells
me that a pack of man-eating Yorkshire terriers have

been reported in midtown Manhattan, and even as I
speak to him I imagine I hear the baying of a dog. I tell
him I can see the Hudson River from my window and not
to worry, I'll be home in about an hour. As it turns out,
the river is the Arno, the window is a framed watercolor,
and I'm not even in Manhattan, having gotten off the IRT
at the wrong stop.

Part of what I wanted to tell you had to do with where
I work and part of it didn't, and you are quite possibly
impatient with me by now, but I have trouble making
certain connections and I no longer remember why it is I
am writing you at all. —JOAN DIDION
Dan Greenburg, N.Y.C.

Dear John

Dear John:
I'm sorry that I have to leave you and our ten children;
but I can't tolerate this kind of behavior. I'm furious! I'm
livid with anger! I'm screaming (inside) with fury! This
letter will upset you. This letter will make you feel miser-
able. I understand. Love Always, Mary
—DR. HAIM G. GINOTT
Mrs. Carol Kanzer, Flushing, N.Y.

Did You Hear the One About . . . ?
Truth is ineluctable. Pinpoint observation impales the
observer while the butterfly eludes the net. *La mode de
jadis comme l'amour d'autrefois s'éteint lentement.* Now
it is the iron taps in the heels of the gentleman's boots
which assault the senses even while the spikes of his para-
mour's plum-colored footwear tap a rapid crescendo of
pops, rapatap rapatap, metal on concrete or carpenter's
nails into flesh. She with the aloe shoes is envelope-white,
slender as a katydid's antenna. A look full into her heart-
shaped face will reveal in one of the lady's eyes a russet
iris flecked with pale gold dots, while in the other an iris

of striking cobalt blue, an astonishingly comic yet not un-common genetic fritz-up. Her cheeks are tipped with the barest crimson blush, framing Pushkin's nose. Of her mouth, I will say nothing. Of her arm, of her *left* arm, I will say only that it is draped in lavender wool and linked with the black serge covering her escort's arm.

Reader! If you could have seen his face the next day when I woke him and confronted him! If you could have heard him burble forth his feeble excuses through morn-ing-caked lips. "Who was that lady?" I roared, I de-manded.

"That was no lady," he managed.

I had already soaked several copies of the *St. Peters-burg Emigré* in slimy kerosene. I lit one. I threw the flaming comic section at him. "That was my wife," he said, and I think he was afraid of me. Perhaps what he said was, "That was my life."

We have no way of knowing. —VLADIMIR NABOKOV
David Axlerod, N.Y.C.

Letter of Resignation
This office is a lousy *pit*
In which I'm sure I'll never *fit*.
The supervisor's always *lit*.
The office manager's a *twit*.
The people here are lacking *wit*.
Their manner makes me throw a *snit*.
I don't like where I have to *sit*.
I'm mad enough to want to *spit*.
I do not like this place a *bit*.
And that, Dear Boss, is why—I *quit!*   —DR. SEUSS
Henry Levinson, N.Y.C.

Dear John
To my dear betrothed Sheine-Sheindel—
You will ask, "Why is Mendel—whom I am to marry

next week—writing to me?" I must begin by informing you that even though you are a feast to the eye and you have shown your handiwork—your sewing and your knitting—and you are kind and good and a considerate woman—and there is none like you in all of Karalevka (and I am sure in Odessa also!)—it has come to pass that I must tell you this, on my word of honor. It is Hodel whom I love. I send you my friendliest wishes and hope —bless the Lord—that you are in the best of health. Amen. Good-by to you. Mendel

—SHOLEM ALEICHEM
Sue Wallach, Roslyn Heights, N.Y.

Weather Forecast
First Witch: "Hail!"
Second Witch: "Hail!"
Third Witch: "Hail!" —WILLIAM SHAKESPEARE
Clinton Sheerr, New Haven, Conn.

A Joke
He stood shivering in front of the window in his shorts, cursing under his breath. She sprawled disconsolately on the bed, not paying much attention to him.

"I hate you," she said. Then, after a moment, "Open another bottle of Calvados."

When he didn't answer, except to mutter another curse under his breath, she looked up.

"Oh, God, I hate you," she said. It was just as Boris had predicted. "You ass, you have a banana in your ear."

Finally he turned away from the window and opened another bottle of Calvados. They drank deeply, not enjoying it.

"What?" he said after a moment.

"I said you have a banana in your ear." She turned away in disgust and drank her Calvados. She lit a cigarette and thought of Boris and what a bore Paris had become.

"What?" he said, lighting a cigarette and sitting on the bed.

"Goddammit," she hissed, "you have a banana in your ear."

How he hated her. He lit another cigarette and, dragging deeply on both cigarettes now, he opened another bottle of Calvados.

"I can't hear you," he said finally, ruefully. "I have a banana in my ear."   —ERICH MARIA REMARQUE
Michael A. Norell, N.Y.C.

Weather Report (Literal Translation)

Word having been brought to Caesar concerning this matter, he determined to make haste in departing from Our Province. He himself was informed by scouts concerning the nature of the danger and determined to undertake a certain plan, whereby the Third Legion would retire to winter quarters, in order that they might be better prepared to face the certain danger of snow (of which he had obtained warning from sources who possessed great knowledge in those matters).

—JULIUS CAESAR
Ellen Garvey, N.Y.C.

Campaign Speech

In the wigwam, wheeling, dealing
Sits with heavy heart our chieftain.
Let's replace him with Dick Nixon
V.P. unto Ike, Dick Nixon.

"With my arms flung high, oh people,
I implore your votes, oh people.
I've a plan to end this sad war.
Can't explain; it's too revealing."

—H. W. LONGFELLOW
Benjamin Hoffman, Monterey Park, Calif.

Recipe

Whan com is Yole with his jolitee,
His myrthe, his reveles, and his brood bountee,
His mistelto and eek his hooly sprigge,
Swich tyme is best to eten yonge pigge.
(A dissh for which Charles Lamb, I have herd seye,
Was woned brennen doun a hous or tweye.)
First scrape and slitt and wassh the litel shote
Til al his smale cors is fresshe and soote.
Than cramm with cestenots the povre felawe,
And herbes fyn til bresting is his mawe,
Anise and swich and spicerie a wisp.
Roost him until his tendre eres been crisp.
Strew al about his plater gerlondes gay,
As certes he were now the Quene of May.
But whan yow stikk an appel in his teth,
A tinie oon been bet, for, be my feyth,
Oon graunt mayhap wole stretcche his comly face,
And folk been stertled be his fiers grimace
And crie out, "Certes, be my faders wigge,
This nas na verray parfit, gentil pigge!"

—GEOFFREY CHAUCER
Mary Catherine O'Connor, Convent, N.J.

Dear John

Dear Dopey, Sneezy, Bashful, Grumpy,
Doc, Happy & Sleepy:
My Prince Has Come! Heigh Ho!

Love,
Snow
—BROS. GRIMM (W. DISNEY)
Richard Miller, N.Y.C.

Marriage Proposal

To Miss Rose Cutpin:
Try as I have to avoid succumbing to the uncontrollable
passions rising in me at the sight of you (with those con-

flicting fires, to which my lacerated heart can testify, hidden beneath that seemingly cool brow so reminiscent of your father riding off to war leaving my mother looking after him quietly contemplating the flutterings of that life beneath her bosom which my small child hand was already aware of as I stood manfully by her side but which she successfully hid from his willingly blind eyes long before his thoughts of you became legitimate reality as the perpetration of his seed, fires once again burning through my family with their insatiable need for vindication and power once so unattainable and now in need of our hereditary strength to refuel), I find myself irresistibly drawn into the vortex of your being and inevitably committed to requesting, with full knowledge of the anguish it must assuredly entail, that you become my wife. Thank you for your consideration. —WILLIAM FAULKNER

Thelma J. Shinn, Bronx, N.Y.

"But Nobody Does Anything About It"

SCENE: *Porch and lawn of a small house, somewhere in the South. The wife (Jo Van Fleet) is rocking on the porch; the husband (E. G. Marshall) is mowing the lawn.*

WIFE: Ahthuh, Ah declayuh, this is thuh *hotte*s' summuh in all mah *memory!* (*Examining outdoor thermometer.*) Ah *sway*uh—uh hunned an' *two!* In thuh *shay*de!

HUSBAND: Don' look lahk it's gonna let up none, April Mae.

WIFE: Tru-uh wuhds wuh nevuh spoke! Whyn'chew come up heah an' have uh duh*lic*ious glassa col' *lem*onade? (*Husband sits on porch glider, which squeaks.*) Yew *prom*ised to awl that gliduh las' week, Ahthuh! An' Ah *dew* lahk to keep up thuh uh*men*ities? (*Pouring lemonade.*) Faw instance, *lem*onade's much maw re*fresh*in' in crystal glasses—Mama taught me that! Whah, Ah couldn' *bring* mahself to suhve *lem*onade in ole Krayuft jelly jahz, lahk Emmuh Juhnine Sahgent! Oh, Mama made shuwah Ah wuz uh lady in evuh re*spec'*. (*Laughing reminiscence.*) But that didn't keep thuh boys from buzzin' roun' *me!* "Lahk bees roun' huhny"—Mama said that *awl* thuh tahm. . . . *Yew* remembuh! (*Husband nods, turns on nearby radio.*)

RADIO ANNOUNCER: An' it's gonna *stay* 'bove a hunnud degrees faw 'lease anuthuh fowah days.

—HORTON FOOTE
Gloria Ullman, Los Angeles, Calif.

Marriage Proposal
It's Tuesday and I'm busy feeding Sarah's pigeons. They eat so many tranquilizer pellets that she hasn't enough money left to feed me any more. And the police are closing this end of the street down for repairs. Will you marry me, Marion, tomorrow perhaps? David can drive me over to Beltsville, since the sight of the water tower there makes me dizzy—so dizzy I can't manage the car and have had several slight accidents. My malevolent vision returned last night. Surely you, if anyone, can break the black web of my confusion. . . . I love you.

—JOHN CHEEVER
Mrs. Susan Shea, Princeton, N.J.

Letter of Resignation
Whanne that Februare with his snowes ywette and slushe
Cometh to city and werkers werey,
Sum wolde gon on pilgrimages to sunnye climbs.
I am wun and I resigne.   —GEOFFREY CHAUCER
Rosemary Bascome, Shelter Island, N.Y.

Dear John
As the marriage was impending, deep inside methought
of ending,

Ending dear betrothal soon to be naught but forgotten
    lore.
Here, in sad throes of expressing what, the while, I'd
    been repressing,
That I find thee quite depressing and thy comp'ny but a
    bore.
" 'Tis all over now," I whisper. "No more passion, like
    before."
I will see thee—Nevermore!   —EDGAR ALLAN POE
                Marlene Lewis, Southfield, Mich.

Dear John

Dear Tran Van Hung: You're a disaster
Herewith your severance piaster   —OGDEN NASH
                James F. O'Connor, N.Y.C.

Sermon

Some may consider it presumptuous of me to admonish
you that "Thou shalt not commit adultery." After all, one
must consider the historical precedents. On the other
hand, the edict is not as clear-cut as the Supreme Court
and the Spiro Agnews would suggest. Still, consider the
alternatives. If you do commit adultery, the commitments
must necessarily be honored if we are to maintain our
status quo among nations. Even ante *status quo,* precipi-
tate withdrawal could injure innocent parties. But who is
innocent in such a situation? The inferiority complexities
may be the root of the dilemma. Whether or not you
commit adultery, let us pray you do the right thing.

                —MAX LERNER
                Jack Paul, Brooklyn, N.Y.

Dear John

Dear John: Someone there is who doesn't love you all.
                —ROBERT FROST
                Ardian Gill, N.Y.C.

Recipe

Ingredients: Curds, whey, blackbirds (24), water (a pail), lamb (a little), rye (one pocketful), piggies (3, little), pease porridge (cold), sugar, spice, bread, honey, pickled peppers, pumpkin shell. Directions: Pat-a-cake, pat-a-cake, rub-a-dub-dub. To test: stick in thumb, pull out plum. Keeps very well. —MOTHER GOOSE

Tom Morrow, N.Y.C.

Weather Report

There'll be white clouds in a blue sky.
A lovers' sun will shine warmer
to a high of twenty
(the wind was warmer when I was twenty)
Colder tonight, colder
in my lonely frozen bed.
The barometer is steady though the waves sigh sobs
and seagulls cry in the rolling mist.
(No rain expected in this loveless desert.)
There's a cloud over the sea
as lonesome as the wind. —ROD MCKUEN

Edward Lense, Columbus, Ohio

A Commercial

Jeeves regarded the young master as he slumped in the chair, spats awry and moustache adroop. "Shall I pour the usual restorative, sir?" "A stiff one, Jeeves. Bourbon and water." "Water?" Jeeves' eyebrow twitched. Bertie shot his cuffs and bristled, "Why *not* water?" He meant it to sting. "What's the bloody matter with water?" "With all due respect to the master," said Jeeves, "I only wish to reiterate that things go better with Coke."

—P. G. WODEHOUSE

Helene Ellner, Richland, Wash.

☞ *"Here Lies Alexander Portnoy . . ."*

"Here Lies Alexander Portnoy: Alone at Last"

Above, monumental prose. Competitors were invited to submit apposite epitaphs for well-known persons—living, dead, or fictional.

Repeats: Grave situations, bad plots, and prevaricators (Here lies Pinocchio) abounded. Mae West: "Come Up and See Me Sometime"; Timothy Leary: "Last Trip" or "Keep Off the Grass"; Dean Martin: "Hic! Jacet"; and "R.I.P." Torn and Van Winkle.

"Here Lies Elizabeth Taylor Hilton Wilding Todd Fisher Burton, Beloved Wife, Beloved Wife, Beloved Wife, Beloved Wife, Beloved Wife"

DANTE: "It's a Nice Place to Visit, But I Wouldn't Want to Live Here"

H. Slavitz, N.Y.C.

"The Grateful Dead Wish to Thank Everyone Who Made This Occasion Possible"

Lew Powell, Greenville, Miss.

"Here Lies Mick Jagger . . . Gathering Moss" *

BETSY ROSS: "Betsy's to Heaven!"

Rees Behrendt, N.Y.C.
*Ellen Maltz, Brooklyn, N.Y.

1. "   "   —MARCEL MARCEAU

2. Ajctcp Rm Rfc Jyqr   —STEPHEN SONDHEIM

Howard Gradet, Baltimore, Md.

WRONG-WAY CORRIGAN: 2001–1910

Thomas Schweitzer, Queens Village, N.Y.

"The Management of the Polish Roman Catholic Cemetery Is Proud to Present—Princess Lee Radziwill"

"Here Lie Sleepy, Sneezy, Doc, Dopey, Grumpy, Happy, and Bashful. Don't Trip Over the Mound"

Tom Morrow, N.Y.C.

GEROLD FRANK: "The Ghost Writer's in the Sky"

JAMES RADO and JEROME RAGNI: "From Hair to Eternity"

Alfred Uhry, N.Y.C.

"Kyle Rote—And Having Writ Moved On"

Micky and Jerry Josephs, Forest Hills, N.Y.

"Be It Dust to Dust or Ashes to Ashes Whichever Your Choice, It's What Ogden Nash Is"

Richard Allen, N.Y.C.

JACQUES BREL: "You Can Change the Name of That Show Now"

Donald Wigal, N.Y.C.

"Garson's Gone and Gabriel's Got Her"
>*Howard Haines, N.Y.C.*

TOULOUSE-LAUTREC: "Make Mine a Short Bier"

MARY ANN MADDEN: "No Contest"
>*Michael Deskey, N.Y.C.*

FALSTAFF: "The Fat Is in the Fire"

ICARUS: "Good to the Last Drop"
>*Stanley Rosenbaum, Florence, Ala.*

ANDY WARHOL: "Underground, Movie Director"
>*Alec McCowen, N.Y.C.*

MARY BAKER EDDY: "I Am Not Here!"
>*David E. Gill, Middletown, N.J.*

"Here Lies Mario Andretti—Failure to Signal—Five Points."
>*Kathleen Dick, Northport, N.Y.*

COUNT BASIE: "No More Times"
>*Sheldon Biber, Union City, N.J.*

"Here Lies Heidi" (Heidi Wouldn't Lie?)
>*Carol Drew, Palisades Park, N.J.*

ABE FORTAS: "There's No Justice in This"
>*Margery Cunningham, Columbia, Miss.*

"Beneath This Plot Is Jim Garrison—Behind It Is the CIA"
>*Michael Boardman, N.Y.C.*

"R.I.P. Henry Ford: Horseman, Pass By"
>*Kathrin Perutz, Great Neck, N.Y.*

PETER STUYVESANT: "Here I Lie With One Foot in the Grave"

"Vacancy: Jacques Brel Is Alive and Well . . ."
Ann Cohen, Bayonne, N.J.

CHIEF SITTING BULL: "The Buck Stops Here"
Marshall Karp, N.Y.C.

"Here Leis Don Ho"
Jeffrey Dames, Long Island City, N.Y.

"Here Lies Elizabeth the Queen: Original Production Conceived and Directed by Henry Tudor and Anne Boleyn"
Jay R. Wolf, N.Y.C.

GWEN VERDON: "There's Gotta Be Something Better Than This"
Gary Westby-Gibson, Glen Rock, N.J.

LAUREL & HARDY: "Well, Here's Another Nice Mess You've Got Us Into"
Cate Ryan, N.Y.C.

STEPHEN SONDHEIM: "With Acknowledgments to the Listener"
Neil Shand, N.Y.C.

MARQUIS DE SADE: "Thy Rod and Thy Staff Shall Comfort Me"
Susan Friedman, New Haven, Conn.

BETTY CROCKER: "Please Omit Flours"
June Padgett, Kansas City, Mo.

BARBARA WALTERS: "Yesterday"
Mrs. Carol Mitchell, Sylacauga, Ala.

MOZART: "Decomposing"
Robert Schleeweiss, Whitestone, N.Y.

ANNE HATHAWAY: "I Laid Me Down with a Will"
Harriett D. McMahon, Arlington, Va.

☞ *Famous First Words*

"Well, she won't have Dick Nixon kicking around any more"

Above, the imagined first words of the President. Competitors were invented to invent famous first words for any well-known person.

Repeats: Womb service, upper berths, and labor negotiations were popular conceptions. Other reproductions: "One small step for man . . ."—Neil Armstrong; "Dr. Livingstone, I presume?"—Sir H. M. Stanley; "This is Life?"—Henry Luce; "I did it my way"—Julius Caesar; "I'm beginning to see the light"—Thomas Edison; "Dada"—Marcel Duchamp; "I shall return!"—Oedipus; "Tsk! Tsk!"—Margaret Sanger; "And now, for my next trick . . ."—H. Houdini; "Chapter Two"—B. Spock; and "——— ———"—Harpo Marx.

"Yoknapatawphawawa"
—WILLIAM FAULKNER
Dale Anderson, N.Y.C.

"Now, if I can just remember what she looks like . . ."
—OEDIPUS REX
Mary Ann Code, N.Y.C.

"Merry Christmas"
—J. CHRIST
James F. Daly, Passaic, N.J.

"And that's the way it is, Tuesday, November 4th, 1916"
—WALTER CRONKITE
Michael Leach, N.Y.C.

"Tell Virginia"   —SANTA CLAUS
Albert G. Miller, N.Y.C.

"This little piggy went to market, this little piggy stayed home . . ."   —GEORGE HORACE GALLUP
Domingo A. Rodrigues, N.Y.C.

"You know, my mother rather resembles the evening spread out against the sky"   —T. S. ELIOT
Leslie Tonner, N.Y.C.

"A bit of talcum
Is always walcum"   —OGDEN NASH
Robert Hudson, Ridgewood, N.J.

"I, Oscar Levant, being of sound mind and body, do hereby bequeath . . ."

Herb Sargent, N.Y.C.

"Howl!"   —ALLEN GINSBERG
Mrs. Carol Lowe, Riverdale, N.Y.

"Moo Goo Gai Pan"   —CONFUCIUS
Jared Weinberger, Morristown, N.J.
D. Davis, Huntington, N.Y.

"Me, Claudius"

Henry Morgan, N.Y.C.

"If I have but one life to live, let me live it as a blond"
—GEORGE WALLACE
Christopher Hood, Rock Hill, S.C.

"My mother thanks you, my father thanks you, my sister thanks you, and I thank you"   —GEORGE M. COHAN
Marci Bernstein, Matawan, N.J.
Mary Ann Rice, Bronxville, N.Y.

"What day is this?"

—TUESDAY WELD
George Malko, N.Y.C.

"This could be the start of something big"

—JACKIE GLEASON
Norton J. Bramesco, N.Y.C.
Jeanne Stoller, N.Y.C.
Michele Evans, N.Y.C.

"I am lying here now on the white bed. . . . I've been here forever . . . or at least it seems forever . . . perhaps it is never. . . . I'll go back. . . ."

—SAMUEL BECKETT
Ronald J. Bohn, Los Angeles, Calif.

"Dooby Dooby Doo"

—FRANK SINATRA
Alan Kaltman, Highland Park, N.J.
Alan M. Novich, Chicago, Ill.

"Hello, Muddah. Hello, Faddah" —ALLAN SHERMAN
Marshall Karp, N.Y.C.

"Now you see me, now you don't" —JUDGE CRATER
Gene Oberg, Richmond, Va.

"Crawl. Crawl. Cross. Slide. Crawl"

—ARTHUR MURRAY
Rees Behrendt, N.Y.C.

"☆☆½"

—WANDA HALE
Mrs. S. S. Klein, North Caldwell, N.J.

"*That* was a Jewish mother?" —DAN GREENBURG
John Gregory Dunne, Los Angeles, Calif.

"I want my mummy" —BORIS KARLOFF
Mrs. Paul Stein, N.Y.C.
Arthur J. Cunningham, N.Y.C.

"Hello. Hello. Hello. Hello. Hello. Hello. Hello"

—SNOW WHITE
Tom Morrow, N.Y.C.

"Cogito Ergo Sum"
—UNIVAC
Neil Leonard, N.Y.C.

"That was disgusting"
—TI-GRACE ATKINSON
Patti Deutsch, N.Y.C.

"Here goes nothing"
—SONNY TUFTS
R. MacKinnon, N.Y.C.

"Is that all there is?"
—PEGGY LEE
Mrs. F. Brancaccio, Huntington, N.Y.
Peter B. Spivak, Detroit, Mich.

"Call me Ishmael"

John Rasor, Pittsfield, N.Y.

"M-m-m-m-m-m-Mama"
—ETHEL MERMAN
Kenny Solms, Los Angeles, Calif.

"And furthermore . . ."
—MARTHA MITCHELL
Hank Levinson, N.Y.C.
Angelo R. Papa, Trenton, N.J.

"I'll cry today"
—LILLIAN ROTH
Janet Ellner, Bronx, N.Y.

"What! You haven't even seen *Man of La Mancha* once?"
—DON QUIXOTE
Alan Levine, Amityville, N.Y.

"I've looked at life from both sides now"
—JUDY COLLINS
JoAnn Wexler, Stanford, Calif.

☞ The Game of Dan Greenburg

Dan Greenburg, Dan McGrew, Robert W. Service, Army Archerd, Robin Hood, Friar Tuck, Thelonious Monk, King Kong, King Arthur, King James, King Family, Swiss Family Robinson, Sugar Ray Robinson, Edward G. Robinson, Little Caesar, Sid Caesar, Imogene Cocoa, James Coco, Katharine Hepburn, Audrey Hepburn, Philip Hepburn, Philip Barry, Jr., Efrem Zimbalist, Jr., Nora Ephron, Dan Greenburg.

Above, some free associations patterned after those by Dan Greenburg in his book, *Chewsday*. Competitors were invited to submit a stream of unconsciousness beginning with any familiar name, ending with that name and employing a total of exactly twenty-five well-known names.

Gertrude Stein, Alex Rose, Rose Kennedy, Dr. Rose Franzblau, Eleanor Roosevelt, Franklin D. Roosevelt, Samuel Rosenman, Peter de Rose, Porfirio Rubirosa, Teddy Roosevelt, Mexicali Rose, Alice Roosevelt Longworth, Julius Rosenberg, Ethel Rosenberg, Pete Rozelle, Lou Groza, Bobby Rosengarden, Rose Marie, Gypsy

Rose Lee, Rosie O'Grady, Abie's Irish Rose, Second Hand Rose, Mae Bush, Gertrude Stein.

Max E. Lynne, Brooklyn, N.Y.

Joan Rivers, Gerald Ford, John Dickson Carr, Francis Scott Key, Diana Dors, Alexander Graham Bell, Sir Robert Peel, William of Orange, Elijah Pitts, Frank Field, Lucille Ball, Bert Parks, Veronica Lake, Ethel Waters, Charles B. Flood, Larry Gates, Wiley Post, Thomas Mann, Tyrone Power, Ray Bloch, Edith Head, Ken Strong, Karen Steele, Lloyd Bridges, Joan Rivers.

Norton J. Bramesco, N.Y.C.

James Mason, Jeane Dixon, Russell Lynes, Beatrice Straight, Nevil Shute, Dyan Cannon, Lucille Ball, Lon Chaney, Abraham Lincoln, Felix Frankfurter, Orson Bean, Chili Williams, Claude Pepper, Rose Marie, Russell Sage, Stephen Wise, Learned Hand, Elizabeth Taylor, Leon Bibb, Forrest Tucker, Helen Twelvetrees, Mary Garden, House Jameson, John Bricker, James Mason.

Edward Reisine, Commack, N.Y.

Lady Godiva, Max Baer, Pooh, Christopher Robin, Batman, Dracula, Bram Stoker, Betty Furness, Nat "King" Cole, Hugo Black, Felix Frankfurter, Philip Hamburger, John Philip Sousa, Hal March, June Walker, H. Ryder Haggard, Don Juan, Satan, Lillian Hellman, Robert Sherwood, Robin Hood, Clara Bow, Gloria Swanson, Buff Cobb, Lady Godiva.

M. M. Richardson, N.Y.C.

John Updike, Hans Brinker, Peggy Fleming, Ian Fleming, James Bond, John James Audubon, Christopher Robin, A. A. Milne, Martin Milner, Lilly Daché, Leslie Caron, Leslie Neilsen, Birgit Nilsson, Rudolf Bing, Don Cherry, Don January, Fredric March, John Philip Sousa,

Susan Sontag, Stephen Sondheim, Harold Prince, King John, John Bunny, Peter Rabbit, John Updike.

Arnold Cover, Sarasota, Fla.

Andy Warhol, Glen Campbell, Soupy Sales, Johnny Cash, Frank Buck, Mr. Chips, Robert Donat, Juan Valdez, Isadora Duncan, Vanessa Redgrave, Yorick, Captain Horatio Hornblower, Louis Armstrong, Lena Horne, Lotte Lenya, Mack the Knife, Jack the Ripper, Jack, Jill, Fanny Hill, Fanny Brice, Baby Snooks, Sonny Tufts, Ultra Violet, Andy Warhol.

Richard Moss, N.Y.C.

William Sydney Porter, Henry I, Henry II, Henry III, Henry IV, Henry V, Henry VI, Henry VII, Henry VIII . . .

Bradford Willett, Fox Lake, Ill.

Dr. No, James Bond, Smith & Wesson, Peter Gunn, Rod la Rocque, Lewis Stone, Arlene Judge, Clement Haynsworth, Pigmeat Markham, Petunia Pig, Fleur Cowles, Julius Monk, Mike Downstairs, Stepin Fetchit, Gunga Din, Ethel Waters, Joan Rivers, Arthur Lake, Blondie, Goldilocks, Elaine Stritch, Cardinal Cooke, Julia Child, Benjamin Spock, Dr. No.

Giac Bozzi, N.Y.C.

. . . Lemuel Gulliver, Robinson Crusoe, Jack Webb, Donald Duck, Daffy Dean . . .

Neil D. Isaacs, Knoxville, Tenn.

. . . Giacometti, The Thin Man, Sydney Greenstreet, Alley Oop, M Graw-Hill, Dale Carnegie . . .

Roy Comart, N.Y.C.

. . . Minnesota Fats, Minnie the Moocher, Cab Calloway, Heidi, Howard Hughes . . .

Mrs. Geraldine Rizzolo, West Orange, N.J.

. . . Franz Liszt, Adrian Messenger, Garcia, Greer Garson, Miniver Cheevy.

Justin and Susan Frank, Boston, Mass.

. . . Howard Hughes, The Phantom, The Lone Ranger . . .

Harvey Chipkin, N.Y.C.

. . . Thomas Jefferson, Jefferson Airplane, Plain Dealer, Cleveland Amory, Amy Vanderbilt, Etta Kett . . .

Dane Knell, N.Y.C.

. . . Florence Nightingale, Sister George, Clarabelle Cow, Louis Pasteur, Tony Pastor, Norman V. Peale, Beatrice Lillie.

Rees Behrendt, N.Y.C.

Geoffrey Chaucer, Boom-Boom Geoffrian, Curtis LeMay . . .

Kathleen Goldhirsch, Brooklyn, N.Y.

. . . Patty Duke, John Wayne, Wayne Newton, Cookie Lavaggetto, Sugar Ray Robinson, Anne Bancroft . . .

M. and S. Brockman, N.Y.C.
E. Saltzman, N.Y.C.

Ashley Montague, Juliet Capulet, Juliet of the Spirits, Alice Ghostley, Bob and Carol and Ted . . .

Betty Forman, New Haven, Conn.

. . . Moon Mullins, Kate Smith, Smith Brothers, Santini Brothers, Van Johnson.

Marshall Karp, N.Y.C.

. . . Charlie Brown, Snoopy, J. Edgar Hoover . . .

Michael Foster, Schenectady, N.Y.
Mary L. Smith, Salamanca, N.Y.

. . . Betty Crocker, China Smith, Charlie Chan, Charlie McCarthy, Woody Allen, Alan Ladd, Lassie . . .

C. and J. Conroy, Oak Harbor, Wash.

. . . John of Gaunt, Twiggy, Penelope Tree, Penelope Ashe, Joan of Arc . . .

Pat Geohegan, New Haven, Conn.

Eartha Kitt, Nicholas Katzenbach, Johann S. Bach, Allegra Kent, Jacques D'Amboise, Frére Jacques, Joyce Brothers . . .

David Diener, Irvington, N.Y.

. . . Dinah Shore, Tyrannosaurus Rex . . .

James Turner, N.Y.C.
Alan Kaltman, Highland Park, N.J.

. . . Tiffany's, Audrey Hepburn, Bambi, Walt Disney, Christmas, Amahl, Menotti, The Medium, Marshall Mc-Luhan.

Dennis Marks, N.Y.C.

. . . Dave DeBusschere, M. De Bakey, Paul Hartman, Paul Newman, Minnesota Fats, Hubert Humphrey, R. Nixon, Joe McGinniss, Rex Stout . . .

Brenda Gustin, N.Y.C.

John L. Lewis, Jan Miner, Major Bowes . . .

Bob Barry, N.Y.C.

. . . Daryle Lamonica, Larry Adler.

Michael Bernstein, Matawan, N.J.

. . . Bebe Rebozo, Bozo the Clown, Richard Nixon . . .

Dan Cohen, N.Y.C.

. . . Roy Rogers, Trigger, Melvin Laird . . .

Racket Shreve, N.Y.C.

. . . George Meany, Richard Widmark . . .

Mrs. Dolores Dolan, N.Y.C.

. . . Andrew Jackson, Charlton Heston, Moses, Barbara Rush . . .

Alan Burke, N.Y.C.

. . . Adm. Rickover, Popeye, Olive Oyl, Mario Procaccino . . .

P. Dantschick, Flushing, N.Y.

. . . June Havoc, Mark Rudd . . .

Charles Almon, Brooklyn, N.Y.

. . . Bennett Cerf, Random House, Polly Adler . . .

Richard Lynne, N.Y.C.

. . . Percy Kilbride, Henry VIII . . .

Bruce Adams, Hartford, Conn.

. . . Emerson Boozer, Phil Harris . . .

Dorothy Swagler, N.Y.C.

. . . John Birch, Pine Brothers, Camille . . .

Mrs. June Cleanthes, N.Y.C.

. . . Nina Simone, Harold Pinter, Mongo Santamaria . . .

Andrea Frost, N.Y.C.

. . . Jude the Obscure, Federico Fellini . . .

W. L. Price, Knoxville, Tenn.

. . . Ulysses S. Grant, Ford Foundation . . .

Linda Pape, Philadelphia, Pa.

Donald Duck, Don Ameche, Alexander Graham Bell, Morris Foner, John V. Lindsay, Mayor Richard Daley, Ernie Banks, David Rockefeller, Salmon Chase, Zebulon Pike, "Man Mountain" Dean, Dean Jagger, The Rolling Stones, Moss Hart, Christiaan Barnard, Adam Smith, Yves Saint Laurent, Coco Chanel, Lewis B. Hershey, Roald Amundsen, Richard E. Byrd, Robert H. Finch, Richard M. Nixon, Spiro Agnew, Donald Duck.

Linda H. Heinze, N.Y.C.

John Updike, John and Yoko, John and Mary, Mia and Frank, Frankie and Johnnie, Bonnie and Clyde, Bob and Carol, Ted and Alice, George and Martha, Richard and Liz, Antony and Cleopatra, David and Bathsheba, David and Lisa, Romeo and Juliet, Hero and Leander, Pélléas and Mélisande, Aucassin and Nicolette, Daphnis and Chloë, Abelard and Héloïse, Edward and Wallis, Tony and Margaret, King Henry and Anne, Angela and Piet, Foxy and Ken, John Updike.

Charles M. Maguire, Chevy Chase, Md.

Ava Gardner, Bea Lillie, Seymour Glass, Dino Di Laurentiis, Yma Sumac, Efrem Zimbalist, Gina Lollobrigida, H. Ryder Haggard, Ida Lupino, Jaye P. Morgan, Kaye Ballard, El Greco, Emma Bovary, Enrico Fermi, Ona Munson, Pee Wee Reese, *Cue* magazine, Arlo Guthrie, Esther Williams, Tina Louise, Yul Brynner, Vito Genovese, Xavier Cugat, Wyatt Earp, Zero Mostel, Ava Gardner.

A. T. Hannett, N.Y.C.
Mrs. S. P. Cohen, Philadelphia, Pa.

. . . Ernest Hemingway, El Cordobes, Elmo Roper, George Gallup, Man o' War, Lord Nelson . . .

Mrs. Susan Stanfield, Knoxville, Tenn.

Carter Burden, Buddy Rich, George Pal, Fred Friendly, Moms Mabley, William Haddad, Fatha Hines, Mama Leone . . .

Gene Tashoff, Jamaica, N.Y.

. . . Johnny Cash, Cash McCall, Shana Alexander, George Stevens . . .

Dick Adler, N.Y.C.
Michael R. Milano, Fort Belvoir, Va.

. . . Hester Prynne, Lady Chatterley, Lady Winder-mere, Sally Rand, Gypsy Rose Lee, Rosalind, Phoebe Caulfield, Franny Glass, Laurette Taylor . . .

R. Barrett and N. Waddy, Palo Alto, Calif.

. . . Billy Graham, John the Baptist, Salome, Oscar Mayer . . .

Judith Stewart, Lock Haven, Pa.

. . . Charlie Chan, Carol Channing, Dolly Madison, Henrik Ibsen . . .

Mrs. H. H. Gary III, Virginia Beach, Va.

. . . Mary Ann Madden, Lucia di Lammermoor . . .

Mrs. C.E. Schildknecht, Gettysburg, Pa.

☞ I Get Raps Now

G.O.P. RATES WIN
I GET RAPS NOW

Above, anagrams derived from the name Spiro T. Agnew. Competitors were invited to submit up to two anagrams of one well-known name.

Franklin Delano Roosevelt:

   LOVED ELEANOR FIRST; KLAN, NO!

   OVERT FALA DROOLS IN KENNEL

Mrs. Dagmar Geidel, Staten Island, N.Y.

William Randolph Hearst:

   NEWS ARM HAD HILLTOP LAIR

Mavis A. Kaunders, N.Y.C.

Daniel Patrick Moynihan:

   DEM IN A LOAN IN HICK PARTY

   CITY MAN HI IN REP. LAND, A-OK

Hilary J. Fried, Rowayton, Conn.

Albert Einstein:

$$\frac{Rt}{S} = b \frac{t}{\sqrt{IEe}} + en/\frac{n}{i} = AL$$

   TEN ELITE BRAINS

Martin Charnin, N.Y.C.

Norman Vincent Peale:

A LENTEN P.R. MAN——NO VICE!

MEN CAN TAP INNER LOVE

Allan B. Smith, N.Y.C.

Harold Stassen:

LOSER HAS STAND

RAN, LOST——HE'S SAD

Mrs. Paul Stein, N.Y.C.

William Westmoreland:

ARMED MALES——WILL TO WIN

WAR——MILLIONS MEET LAWD

Lee Cross, N.Y.C.

Ernest Hemingway:

"THY MEN SIN!" WE RAGE

MANY WERE THE GINS

William T. Jeanes, Jackson, Miss.

Adolf Hitler:

ILL OF HATRED

TOLD "HEIL" FAR

Thelma Blitz, N.Y.C.

Michelangelo Buonarroti:

O, I'M A LI'L CHERUB, GONE ON ART

LABOR (AMOUR): ON THE CEILING

Robert M. Kramer, Riverdale, N.Y.

Amedeo Modigliani:

O, I'D MADE A GEM IN OIL

ME, DIE? I'D LOOM AGAIN!

Ronni Dumbroff, Rego Park, N.Y.

Piet Mondrian:
> I PAINT MODERN
>
> I.E., NOT DRIP MAN

Edith A. Ehrlich, N.Y.C.

Jacqueline Bouvier Kennedy Onassis:
> YON QUEEN SAILS EVER, I.E., JOB IN D.C. SUNK

Dolores Sutton, N.Y.C.

Stephen Sondheim:
> DEMON! HE PENS HITS
>
> HE HONES MINDS, PET

Marilyn H. Rubin, N.Y.C.

Robert F. Wagner:
> WENT FOR REGRAB

Elaine G. Greene, N.Y.C.

Craig Claiborne:
> CARING BROIL ACE
>
> CRAB IN GLACE ROI

Linda and Larry Zamzok, Brooklyn, N.Y.

Eleanor Rigby:
> A LONE GREY RIB
>
> BE LEARY, RINGO

Beverly Schindler, N.Y.C.

Arnold Palmer:
> MODERN ALL-PAR
>
> REALM? PRO-LAND

Aubrey E. Denney, N.Y.C.

Timothy Leary:

I'M HOLY—TRY TEA

Sheldon Biber, Union City, N.J.

Walter Cronkite:

NETWORK RECITAL

IRK NOT LATE CREW

Sandra Didyk, Westbury, N.Y.

David Brinkley:

VERY AD LIB KIND

ABLY DRIVEN KID

Barbara Israel, N.Y.C.

Barbra Streisand:

DRESS BRAT IN A BRA,

AND STAR BARES RIB

Tom Morrow, N.Y.C.

Charles de Gaulle:

DULLES' REGAL ACHE

HE'S AGED, ALL-CRUEL

Walter G. Leight, Bethesda, Md.

William Shakespeare:

AH, SPAKE I A SWELL RIME

MAWKISH, I PLEASE LEAR

Robert D. Croog, N.Y.C.

Scarlett O'Hara

O RHETT, A RASCAL

LO, TARA'S HER ACT

Mrs. Stanley Charren, Newton Center, Mass.

George A. Hirsch:
GO CHEER HIS RAG!

Jerrold Hickey, Boston, Mass.

Woodrow Wilson:
O LORD, SO NOW W.W. I

O SON, I WOW WORLD!

Mrs. Thomas Mooney, Asbury Park, N.J.

Leonard Bernstein:
ENTERS ROLE IN BAND

BATON RENDERS LINE

Mary E. Lyons, N.Y.C.

Oscar Wilde:
I LACE WORDS

A.R. Papa, Trenton, N.J.

Frank Sinatra:
RANKS IN A FRAT

IRKS AN ART FAN

Mrs. Lenore Tours, Bronx, N.Y.

Alexander Portnoy:
LOX-PRONE AND TEARY

AN EXPERT, LADY, OR NO?

Andrew D. Washton, Brooklyn, N.Y.

George Hamilton:
I MET HER LONG AGO

Mrs. Stuart M. Gustin, N.Y.C.

William Shakespeare:
ME . . . LEAR . . . SPEAK SWAHILI?

William Katz, N.Y.C.

Marc Antony:

COY RANT MAN

CANTY ROMAN

Mrs. F.T. McMahon, Arlington, Va.

Yves St. Laurent:

STYLE NUTS RAVE

Alice Edmunds, N.Y.C.

☞ *"Thank You for the Giant Sea Tortoise"*

"Good Luck to the Drop-out"
"So you've been elected President of the United States!"
"Congratulations to my son-in-law on joining the firm"

Above, unseemly greeting cards for unlikely occasions. Competitors were invited to supply greeting card messages for similarly odd occasions.

"So You've Been Chosen Thane of Cawdor . . ."

David Deutsch, Washington, D.C.

"Watched Your Smoke! Now You're Pope! Congrats!"

Charles M. Maguire, Chevy Chase, Md.

"Congratulations on Your Oscar for Best Cinematography in a Feature-Length, Black-and-White, Foreign-Language, American-made Documentary"

Linda J. Bomba, Elizabeth, N.J.

"Congratulations on Becoming a Spy!"

Mrs. Margaret Wolf, N.Y.C.

"Good Luck on Your Appointment to the CIA"

Manny Schwam, Brooklyn, N.Y.

"So You Made an Ass of Yourself at a Foreign Film Festival!"

Mrs. Helen McMonegal, N.Y.C.

"Sory I Havent Ritten Lately—I Hait Riting"

Alex Tropp, Bayside, N.Y.

"To My Secret Pal on Mother's Day"

John Cunha, Islip, N.Y.

"Sorry to Hear about Your Allergy to Paper Products"

Herb Sargent, N.Y.C.

"Good Luck in the Nuclear Holocaust"

Michael Lynne, N.Y.C.

"Congratulations to the Fascist Pig on His Graduation from Police Academy"

Donald Kaul, Potomac, Md.

"So You've Had a Pre-Frontal Lobotomy!"

Barbara Schein, White Plains, N.Y.

"Well, I'll Be Damned, You Were Excommunicated!"

Paul Bailyn, N.Y.C.

"Sorry About Last Night"

Li Hoffman, Berkeley, Calif.

"On Your First Anniversary—Congratulations to a Wonderful Junta"

Joanna Steichen, N.Y.C.

"Just Operated on Your Hearing"

S. Stecklow, Brooklyn, N.Y.

"Thank You for the Giant Sea Tortoise"

Tom Morrow, N.Y.C.

"Congratulations on Having Your Charge Reduced to Simple Assault"

Jack Brennan, Leonia, N.J.

"Overjoyed to Hear about You and Your Winstons"

Henry Morgan, N.Y.C.

"The Gang at the Office Will Miss You Except for the Business Manager"

Henry W. Levinson, N.Y.C.

"Congratulations to My Son on His Resurrection"

Richard Lynne, N.Y.C.

"Condolences on the Loss of Your Shirt"

Carol Drew, Palisades Park, N.J.

"Congratulations on Being Selected the New Patron Saint of Travel"

Edward J. Walker, N.Y.C.

"Thinking of You as You Picket"

Andrea Ackerly, Manorville, N.Y.

"Hats Off to Your New Hairpiece!"

Harvey M. Sheirr, N.Y.C.

"So You've Moved into a Previously All-White Neighborhood!"

Bruce Bullen, Williamstown, Mass.

"Good Luck with Your New Boomerang: Many Happy Returns!"

Tony Nap, Woodside, N.Y.

"All of Us Here on the Estate Wish You a Speedy Recovery, Uncle"

Larry Nadelman, N.Y.C.
Hilma Wolitzer, Syosset, N.Y.

"Hope Your Recent Illness Was a Pleasant One"

Susan Kantor, N.Y.C.

"Merry Christmas to Apt. 4-F from Your Doorman—This Is Your First Notice"

Allan B. Smith, N.Y.C.

"Sorry I Was Out When You Called, But Kiss the Baby for Me Anyway"

Angelo R. Papa, Trenton, N.J.

"So You Got Change from a Bus Driver!"

Richard Wolff, N.Y.C.

"Pleasure-Pain to You on the Completion of Your Psychoanalysis"

Alfie Mack, N.Y.C.

"May You Rest in Peace"

Pam and Bob Sloane, Paramus, N.J.

☞ *The Bride Wore Black and Selected Shorts*

Me, Natalie and *I, a Woman*
The Night Has a Thousand Eyes with *A Woman's Face*
plus Third Feature *Chafed Elbows*
The Bride Wore Black and Selected Shorts

Above, some unlikely movie marquees. Competitors were invited to submit fortuitous double or triple bills.

Repeats: *Hard Contract* and *Easy Rider;*
Goodbye, Columbus and *Hello, Dolly;*
I Am Curious (Yellow), What Ever Happened to Baby Jane? Heaven Knows, Mr. Allison;
The Grapes of Wrath and *The Wild Bunch;*
Breakfast at Tiffany's and *Dinner at Eight* (with *Duck Soup* and *Animal Crackers*);
Blow-Up, The Red Balloon, and *Breathless;*
A Man for All Seasons with *Salt and Pepper;*
Myra Breckinridge, Funny Girl;
Candy, A Taste of Honey and *How Sweet It Is;*

Salesman and *The Farmer's Daughter;*
Blackboard Jungle and *The Chalk Garden;*
Call Northside 777 and *Sorry, Wrong Number;*
Daddy's Gone a-Hunting with *100 Rifles;*
On the Beach with *The Sand Pebbles* and *True Grit;*
Accident and *Marry Me! Marry Me!;*
The 39 Steps, Staircase, and *Vertigo;*
The Light That Failed and *The Dark at the Top of the
Stairs;*
I Remember Mama and *Monterey Pop;*
*What Did You Do in the War, Daddy, I Was a Male
War Bride;*
One Touch of Venus and *A Farewell to Arms;*
*The Three Faces of Eve, The Good, the Bad, and the
Ugly;*
Chitty Chitty Bang Bang and *Boom:*
Dr. Zhivago and *The Young Interns;*
Prudence and the Pill, Fail-Safe;
For Love of Ivy and *The Seven-Year Itch;*
The King and I with Short Subjects.

GALA REVIVAL——EASTER PARADE

FIGHT PAY TV——THE WRONG BOX

THE THIRTEENTH LETTER——M

Neil P. Jampolis, N.Y.C.

D.O.A.* G.W.T.W.* ZHIVAGO, M.D., and A.M. BECOMES
ELECTRA

James Elson, N.Y.C.
**Morton Gottlieb, N.Y.C.*

BUTTERFIELD 8——1984

SUDDENLY——SUDDENLY LAST SUMMER——LAST SUMMER

THE PRODUCERS——HELP——FIGHT PAY TV

Alan Lipp, Brooklyn, N.Y.

BROKEN ARROW and THE FIXER

SHAME—SHANE

PORTRAIT OF JASON—THE AFRICAN QUEEN

J. B. McFarland, Cambridge, Mass.

FRIENDLY PERSUASION—PAY OR DIE

THE SUN ALSO RISES—THE CURSE OF DRACULA

ROSEMARY'S BABY—YOUNG MAN WITH A HORN

Alexandra Isles, N.Y.C.

GUESS WHO'S COMING TO DINNER?—THE RUSSIANS ARE COMING! THE RUSSIANS ARE COMING!

Coming Next Week: FIFTY MILLION FRENCHMEN

Richard Fithian, N.Y.C.

THE TEN COMMANDMENTS—WITH SIX YOU GET EGGROLL

FREUD—THE INCREDIBLE SHRINKING MAN

Mike Schiffrin, San Francisco, Calif.

THANK YOU ALL VERY MUCH—WELCOME STRANGER

I MARRIED AN ANGEL—I MARRIED A WITCH—TO EACH HIS OWN

Mrs. Edward W. Powell, Jr., N.Y.C.

THE CAT AND THE CANARY—BRIEF ENCOUNTER

THE LIEUTENANT WORE SKIRTS—SUSPICION

Charlotte Curtis, N.Y.C.

THE BALCONY with ROMEO AND JULIET

G. Y. Alexander, N.Y.C.

THE NIGHT THEY RAIDED MINSKY'S—LADIES IN RETIREMENT

Harold Parks, Philadelphia, Pa.

TRIO plus QUARTET—THE MAGNIFICENT SEVEN

Marvin Aledort, N.Y.C.

BUNNY LAKE IS MISSING—BOBBY WARE IS MISSING—WHAT EVER HAPPENED TO AUNT ALICE?—THE INVASION OF THE BODY SNATCHERS

Dick Mendelsohn, N.Y.C.

MELBA—THE TOAST OF NEW ORLEANS

William Tynan, N.Y.C.

THE SHAMELESS OLD LADY Now Playing with THE MAN IN THE WHITE SUIT

Arthur J. Morey, N.Y.C.

THE LAS VEGAS STORY—GOODBYE, MR. CHIPS*

THIRTY SECONDS OVER TOKYO and SAYONARA

Hyman Levy, N.Y.C.
*Preston Jones, New Canaan, Conn.

ACCIDENT with A MAN AND A WOMAN Coming Soon: ROSEMARY'S BABY

Joanna Steichen, N.Y.C.

BROADWAY and 42ND STREET

I MARRIED A WITCH—THAT UNCERTAIN FEELING

Warren G. Harris, N.Y.C.

SEND ME NO FLOWERS—MAKE MINE MINK and I CAN GET IT FOR YOU WHOLESALE

Wilhelmina Ford, Jersey City, N.J.

Boulevard Drive-In Presents: ACCIDENT and WHIPLASH

COOL HAND LUKE and POOR COW

C. Maguire, Chevy Chase, Md.

KHARTOUM plus Cartoons

> *Paul Cantor, San Francisco, Calif.*

STILETTO—DEEP IN MY HEART

GOING MY WAY with THE HITCHHIKER*

> *Marilyn Rubin, N.Y.C.*
> *Allan B. Smith, N.Y.C.*

Last Time Today: TOMORROW NEVER COMES with DARKNESS AT NOON

Delightfully Air-Conditioned: HEAVEN CAN WAIT—HELLO DOWN THERE

> *Raymond Kauders, N.Y.C.*

THE RAZOR'S EDGE and PERSONA

> *Leo Katainen, Saginaw, Mich.*
> *Matthew Golden, Brooklyn, N.Y.*

GRAND HOTEL with ROOM SERVICE

> *Kathi Sheppard, Yardley, Pa.*

A CHILD IS WAITING—INSIDE DAISY CLOVER

WHAT EVER HAPPENED TO AUNT ALICE?—ALICE'S RESTAURANT—IN WHICH WE SERVE

> *Michael Feingold, New Haven, Conn.*

CAMILLE—CALL NORTHSIDE 777—ALFIE

> *Ronald Bohn, Los Angeles, Calif.*

THE FBI STORY—THE BRAVE BULLS

> *Frank O'Heaney, Albany, N.Y.*

KING KONG ESCAPES—DON'T JUST STAND THERE—RUN FOR YOUR LIFE

> *Msgr. Archibald McLees, St. Albans, N.Y.*

BILLY LIAR with THE GREATEST STORY EVER TOLD

> *Diane Davis, Huntington, N.Y.*
> *Joan Gale, N.Y.C.*

DIAL M FOR MURDER——M

> *Roderick Cook, N.Y.C.*

A MAN CALLED PETER——THE PUMPKIN EATER*

THE EGG AND I plus Serial

> *William Jeanes, Jackson, Miss.*
> *Todd Everett, Los Angeles, Calif.*

THERESE AND ISABELLE——GIRL CRAZY

> *Don Tenenblatt, Silver Spring, Md.*

I WAS A COMMUNIST FOR THE FBI——PINKY

> *James Townes III, Minter City, Miss.*

I WANT TO LIVE with A MAN FOR ALL SEASONS

> *Ruth Poley, Kingston, N.Y.*

MYRA BRECKINRIDGE——THE MAN WHO NEVER WAS

> *Dalton Alexander, Urbana, Ohio*

THE MAN IN THE GRAY FLANNEL SUIT with THE FLY

> *Lee Glickstein, Brooklyn, N.Y.*

2001: A SPACE ODYSSEY——Previews of Coming Attractions

> *James Jimirro, N.Y.C.*

THE FOUR POSTER with THE VIRGIN SPRING

> *Ed Schultz, N.Y.C.*

Color: ME, NATALIE——I AM CURIOUS (YELLOW)

> *Charles Rosenberg, Hackensack, N.J.*

ELEPHANT WALK with SARATOGA TRUNK

Paul Elfenbein, N.Y.C.

CAUGHT—HELP

J. Pearlstein, Arlington, Va.

IT'S LOVE I'M AFTER—DARLING—WHERE'S CHARLEY?

Peter Havholm, Mansfield Center, Conn.

THE SHOES OF THE FISHERMAN—8½

Corinne Michel, N.Y.C.

YOU'LL NEVER GET RICH with PENNIES FROM HEAVEN

Emily Cole, N.Y.C.

AN AFFAIR TO REMEMBER with AN ALLIGATOR NAMED
DAISY

Mary LeMieux, New Orleans, La.

SAINT JOAN—Save Free TV

John Trojanowski, Bronx, N.Y.

PARDON MY SARONG and CALL ME MISTER

Steven Mackler, Falls Church, Va.

WHEN WORLDS COLLIDE—GIANT—BLOW-UP

Alan Forsyth, N.Y.C.

I WANT TO LIVE—LA DOLCE VITA

Henry Levinson, N.Y.C.

HALLELUJAH, I'M A BUM and SO'S YOUR OLD MAN

Arnold Cover, Sarasota, Fla.

MICKEY ONE—CAMILLE 2000

John Schiano, Brooklyn, N.Y.

I MARRIED AN ANGEL——THE BLUE ANGEL and I AM CURIOUS (BLUE)

FIVE FINGERS and ROOM FOR ONE MORE

Ralston Hill, N.Y.C.

CALL ME MADAM——CALL ME MISTER——DECISION AT DAWN

Sue Heimann, N.Y.C.

GREETINGS——COUNT DRACULA——YOU ARE WHAT YOU EAT

Diane Ostendorff, N.Y.C.

SHOOT THE PIANO PLAYER and YOUNG MAN WITH A HORN

Carol Schwager, N.Y.C.

FLIPPER and THE SEVENTH SEAL

James Harper, Port Jefferson, N.Y.

BUNNY LAKE IS MISSING and NOBODY WAVED GOODBYE

John Daniels, N.Y.C.

THE MAN IN THE IRON MASK with THE IRON GLOVE and THE IRON PETTICOAT

Tom Morrow, N.Y.C.

GOODBYE, COLUMBUS——GOODBYE, MR. CHIPS——BYE BYE BRAVERMAN——GOODBYE AGAIN

Richard Baxter, Circleville, N.Y.

SNOW WHITE——FACES——PRETTY POISON

George R. Golden, Brooklyn, N.Y.

LADY L plus MADAME X——THE ALPHABET MURDERS

Marie McCullagh, Brooklyn, N.Y.

☞ *The Pie Game*

Figs. 1 and 2. *Annual Expenses*

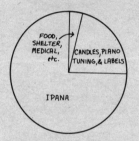

Fig. 1. LIBERACE

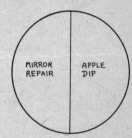

Fig. 2. WICKED QUEEN IN
SNOW WHITE

**Above, the economists' favorite, the money pie.
Competitors were invited to submit pies with
characteristic annual expenses for a well-
known person.**

Repeats: Mrs. Nixon: 80 per cent Other, 20 per cent
Cloth Coats; Myra Breckinridge: 50 per cent Brooks
Brothers, 50 per cent Henri Bendel; Mickey Rooney and
T. Manville: 10 per cent Other, 90 per cent Alimony;
Lady Macbeth: 25 per cent each to Ajax, Comet, Axion,
Clorox; A. Portnoy: 99 per cent Psychiatric Bills, 1 per
cent Mother's Day Cards; Dr. Spock: pies in the form of
Peace Symbols; Flavored and Crusted pies for Mrs. Wag-
ner and Simple Simon; and for Jack Benny, a big empty
pie. Poor dear.

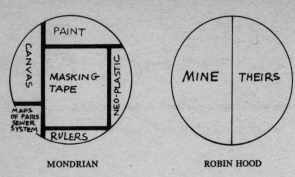

MONDRIAN

ROBIN HOOD

Arnold Rheingold, Seabrook, Md.

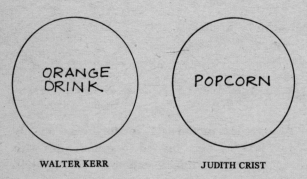

WALTER KERR

JUDITH CRIST

Fran Lebowitz, Convent Station, N.J.

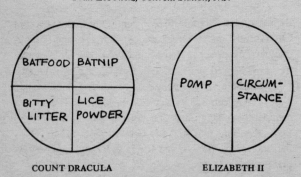

COUNT DRACULA

ELIZABETH II

Mary K. LeMieux, New Orleans, La.

GOD

Janet Coleman Dozer, N.Y.C.

CHRISTOPHER
COLUMBUS

R. J. De Chiara, N.Y.C.

THE DIRECTOR OF
THE PENN CENTRAL

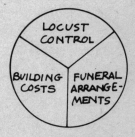

PHARAOH

Andrea Rhodin, Darien, Conn.

HOWARD JOHNSON

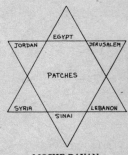

MOSHE DAYAN

Richard S. Rubin, Ithaca, N.Y.

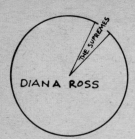

**DIANA ROSS AND
THE SUPREMES**

*Howard Lockman,
Riverside, Ill.*

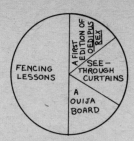

HAMLET

*Suzanne Harrigan,
Minneapolis, Minn.*

LONG JOHN SILVER

*Martin J. Friedman,
Flushing, N.Y.*

ICARUS

*Elaine Kendall,
Princeton, N.J.*

LITTLE ORPHAN ANNIE

*Mrs. S. S. Klein,
North Caldwell, N.J.*

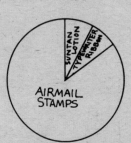

ARNOLD COVER

*Karen Weed, N.Y.C.
Allan Forsyth, N.Y.C.*

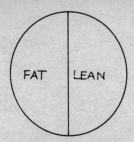

MR. & MRS. J. SPRATT

*J. R. Jacobucci,
Norwalk, Conn.*

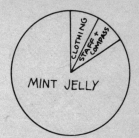

LITTLE BO PEEP

*Ted Demmerle,
New Canaan, Conn.*

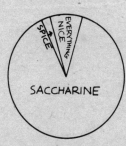

DORIS DAY

*John D. Pollack,
Boston, Mass.*

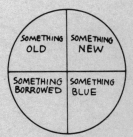

ZSA ZSA GABOR

*Bud Simone,
Bohemia, N.Y.*

LAWRENCE WELK SHOW

*Judith McMahon,
Howard Beach, N.Y.*

SOLOMON GRUNDY

Laura J. Froelich, N.Y.C.

GRETA GARBO

*Cliff Freeman,
Atlanta, Ga.*

CAST OF *Oh! Calcutta!*

*Mrs. Edward W.
Powell, Jr., N.Y.C.*

**THE MAN IN THE MOON
(RECENTLY REVISED
BUDGET)** *Ralston Hill, N.Y.C.*

LIZZIE BORDEN

HOWARD HUGHES

*Thomas Ruffin,
Shreveport, La.*

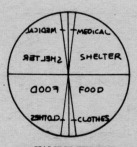

SIAMESE TWINS

*Miles Klein,
Belle Harbor, N.Y.*

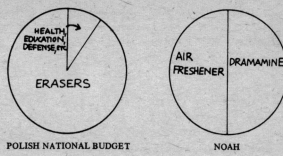

POLISH NATIONAL BUDGET   NOAH

Arthur Cooper, N.Y.C.

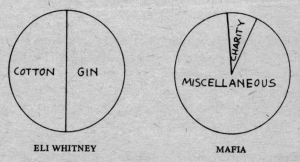

ELI WHITNEY   MAFIA

Marshall Karp, N.Y.C. [1]

[1]Incidentally, many of these Competitions are based on old parlor games and can be readapted quite nicely. "The Pie Game," for example, is great fun. You make the pie, label only the sections, and *then* everyone guesses who it represents. Or whom. And then you all go to the seashore.

☞ *Ignore*
"Off Duty" Signs . . .

The visitor to Manhattan is urged to enjoy an evening stroll in Central Park. . . .

Under no circumstances should tourists tip taxi drivers in excess of the fare registered on the meter. Drivers resent being so patronized, and for this reason have placed a glass partition between themselves and passengers. Ignore "off duty" signs, which are designed to confuse. . . .

Above, excerpts from *Tips to Tourists: A Singular Guide to New York*. Competitors were invited to contribute to this compendium of misinformation.

Resist the impulse to offer money when approached by children handing out orchids on the streets of Manhattan. These children expect nothing more than a warm smile and a pleasant thank you in return and would become frightened and confused by the offer of money.

The tourist is advised to be wary of phony panhandlers lurking in doorways. Members of New York's real hard-core poverty group walk openly through the streets and are known as models. They are easily recognized by their obviously emaciated condition, blank expressions, and large pocketbooks in which they carry their few earthly possessions. However, since they are too proud to beg, the tourist must take the initiative when offering a few coins for a substantial meal.

The visitor should not become embarrassed or frightened upon losing his way in Manhattan's complex subway system. Indeed, he is especially fortunate if this happens during the "rush hour" when many people are available to aid him. By stopping any commuter and asking him for directions, the visitor will be told distinctly and emphatically where to go.

Any experienced traveler knows that in some primitive areas the natives are willing to trade with tourists. Such an area is New York's Greenwich Village, in which the natives, known as hippies, adorn themselves with many strands of multicolored beads. These are actually a means of trade and make wonderful souvenirs. They will be eagerly exchanged with the tourist upon his presentation of such obviously unavailable items as: combs, scissors, soap, and deodorant.

Mrs. Dorothy Wiemart, Brooklyn, N.Y.

The kind of (subway) ride to expect is indicated by the rating on the front of the train:

    A—Great Ride
    BB—Not Bad Ride
    B—Not Too Bad Ride
    C—Fair Ride
    D—Just a Ride
    E—Not a Good Ride at All
    F—Bad Ride
    K—Don't Get on This Train

Martin Charnin, N.Y.C.

Native New Yorkers affectionately call their husky police officers "bigs." If you want to ask one of New York's Finest for directions, greet him with "Hello, big," and ask the way to your destination. He'll tell you where to go.

Patricia Smith, N.Y.C.

Since many movies are filmed in the actual streets of New York, should you by chance come upon what appears on the surface to be a robbery or a mugging, do not interfere and ruin the shooting. Stay well to one side of the action until it is played out, and then you may applaud.

Daniel Cohen, Cambridge, Mass.

Please report any restaurant having cats on the premises to the Health Department. Cats are illegal. Do not report mice, roaches, or rats. They are not illegal.

Aristides Pappidas, N.Y.C.

A Must: Port Authority Bus Terminal. This pleasure dome for the traveler boasts cuisine acclaimed by Craig Claiborne, rest rooms by Craig's wife.

Dorothy L. Herrmann, N.Y.C.

Searching for something pleasant in prints and photographs with which to line the breakfast nook or children's room? Any of the small bookshops that line 42nd Street or Broadway is an excellent source. Ask the clerk for his under-the-counter specials.

Ed Gilbert, N.Y.C.

Tips for Motorists: It is against New York City law to use directional turn signals while driving, as they distract cab drivers and policemen. Horns are used instead.

Robert B. Merkin, Washington, D.C.

The most conveniently located place to obtain theater intermission cocktails is the Bar Association of the City of New York, 44th Street between Broadway and Sixth Avenue.

B. De Fren, N.Y.C.

It is the custom to greet your local policeman in the continental manner, with a kiss on both cheeks.

Nicholas Hartmann, N.Y.C.

. . . Our Wall Street . . . near Chinatown was erected by the Chinese in 1894. The giant fifteen-foot wall surrounds the area, blocking it off from the rest of Manhattan. In this self-governing area money is not used, but the old barter system is still in operation.

Marv Wolfman, Flushing, N.Y.

Audience participation is no longer confined to off-Broadway. At all uptown theaters, audiences are now expected to argue with the actors, shout down other spectators, and remove all clothing by the first intermission at the latest. At the Metropolitan Opera, however, it is customary only to join in the choruses, and retain furs and jewelry.

Roderick Cook, N.Y.C.

ENTERTAINMENT FOR THE KIDDIES: THEATER: The Boys in the Band—a merry musical romp about a teen-age symphony orchestra at Boys Town; *Geese*—a charming ballet based on the adventures of "Little Goosey Gander" and her mischievous chums. FILMS: *The Killing of Sister George*—the inspiring tale of a young nun who makes a "killing" on the stock market and uses the proceeds to build an orphanage for young girls; *The Queen*—a remarkable historic documentary that captures all the color and pageantry of modern court life; *The Fox*—Walt Disney has never been better; *The Sergeant*—the warm, human side of life in a military academy . . .

Jim Black, N.Y.C.

One out of eight New Yorkers is on welfare and travels free on the subways. If you have bought a token, you are automatically entitled to a seat. Approach anyone seated and say: "I'm not on welfare like you. I paid my way. Please give me your seat."

B. Moore, N.Y.C.

Taken from the Manhattan Yellow Pages, 1969: Manhattan Address Locator. To locate avenue addresses, take the address, cancel the last figure, divide by two, add or subtract the key number below. The answer is approximately the nearest numbered cross street. To find addresses on numbered cross streets, remember—numbers increase east or west from 5th Avenue which runs north-south.

Sandra Jackson, Philadelphia, Pa.

Don't Miss: the quaint charm of a number of hotels which line the Bowery. For a substantially reduced rate, the visitor may enjoy all the luxuries of the more expensive hotels, along with the proximity to a large colony of executives populating the area.

Steven W. Wolfe, N.Y.C.

New Yorkers are among the friendliest people in the world and are always interested in newcomers' opinions of their city. When asked by a native how you are enjoying your stay, always reply: "It's a nice place to visit, but I wouldn't want to live here."

Rosemary Shevlin, N.Y.C.

☞ *The East Village Social Register*

The East Village Social Register
The Wit and Wisdom of Enzo Stuarti

Above, nominees for "Shortest Book of the Year" Award. Competitors were invited to submit titles for similarly brief volumes.

Repeats: *Military Strategy* by G. A. Nasser; *Best Plays of 1971* by John Simon; *Onassis Budget Housekeeping; The "Oh! Calcutta!" Pattern Book; The Phyllis Diller Beauty Book; The Faith of Madelyn Murray O'Hair; Competitions We've Lost* by Sargent, Greenburg, Morrow, and Cover; *Quotations from Harpo Marx; The Howard Hughes Picture Book; 400 Years of German Humor; The Films of Bela Darvi; Inside Monaco; Who's Who in Lapland; My Life with Ethel* by Ernest Borgnine; *Namath on Business; Charisma* by Nixon; and *New York on $5 a Day.*

What I'm Going to Do, I Think—RICHARD M. NIXON
Rob Voight, McLean, Va.

Sing Along with Yma Sumac

                                       Lee Bailey, N.Y.C.

The Ayn Rand Joke Book

                         Alan Foster Friedman, N.Y.C.

Popes Say the Darnedest Things

                         Mrs. Esther Blitz, Passaic, N.J.

The Light Verse of Susan Sontag

                         Edwin R. Kammin, N.Y.C.

At Ease with Agnew: The Story I Tell My Friend

                         Enoch Landie, Cambridge, Mass.

Richard Nixon Speaks His Mind

                         Thomas Klunzinger, Detroit, Mich.

Sincerely Yours, Al Capp

                         Clint Cochran, Sacramento, Calif.

Pensées—RAQUEL WELCH

                         John B. Hapgood, Quogue, N.Y.
                         Albert Weiner, North Chatham, N.Y.

The Lasting Influence of the Maharishi Mahesh Yogi

                         Renee Pennington, East Elmhurst, N.Y.

The Reign of Edward VIII

                         Mrs. Mitchell Kern, Midland, Miss.
                         Michael Deskey, N.Y.C.

Nobody Knows My Name—NEIL ARMSTRONG

                         Sue Hackenkamp, McCook, Neb.

The Radical Thoughts of David Eisenhower

                         Richard Lynne, N.Y.C.

Living with Failure—MIKE NICHOLS

> *Arnold Cover, Sarasota, Fla.*
> *Mary Sweenie, Pittsburgh, Pa.*

Making It—EUGENE MCCARTHY

> *Ellen M. Violett, N.Y.C.*

The Best of Harold Robbins

> *Mrs. Clare Weiner, North Chatham, N.Y.*

The Furious Passage of Lillian Gish

> *Tom Morrow, N.Y.C.*

Ireland: A Study of the Emerging Christian Ethic

> *Alison Owings, Washington, D.C.*

Beloved Cabbie

> *American Hamburger League, New Theatre, N.Y.C.*

How I Got My Job—ARTHUR OCHS SULZBERGER

> *Edwin B. Stern, N.Y.C.*

Days in June—LOWELL

> *Diana Newman, Washington, D.C.*

Baby and Child Care—W. C. FIELDS

> *Paul King, Toronto, Canada*
> *Robert Schwarz, Monrovia, Liberia*

GRACE KELLY'S *Give Me the Simple Life*

> *Marel Harayda, Mamaroneck, N.Y.*

Advertisements for Myself—J. D. SALINGER

> *King Morgan, Jr., Washington, D.C.*
> *Leon Bing, Los Angeles, Calif.*

I Never Met a Man I Didn't Like—ALEXANDER WOOLL-
COTT

> Alice Kowal, Mount Prospect, Ill.

Forging the Grand Coalition—MARCHI

> Robert E. Duffy, N.Y.C.

Happy Boyhood Memories—EUGENE O'NEILL

> George L. River, M.D., Marshfield, Wis.

The Making of the Vice President, 1968

> Kenneth Paul, Concord, N.H.

The Comedy of Sparta

> Cindi Mintz, N.Y.C.

Svetlana Alliluyeva and Anatoly Kuznetsov on Loyalty

> Joanna Steichen, N.Y.C.

Making Democracy Work—NGUYEN VAN THIEU

> Mary L. McNulty, N.Y.C.

Architecture: Relevance and Variety—LEVITT

> Dr. L. Tiefer, Fort Collins, Colo.

My Father—PHILIP ROTH

> I. Spedet, N.Y.C.
> B. Blum, N.Y.C.

Pauses by Pinter

> Robert Lantz, N.Y.C.

How to Win the Confidence of the Electorate—HAROLD
WILSON

> Tony Willis, London, England

Good Times—FYODOR DOSTOEVSKI

Bill Wenk, Brooklyn, N.Y.

The Herpetology of Ireland

David Shulman, N.Y.C.
Wayne Childers, Detroit, Mich.

The Military Mind

Leslie Harwood-Jones, Brooklyn, N.Y.

Preparing an Airtight Case for the Prosecution—JIM GARRISON

Bob White, N.Y.C.

Chats with Greta Garbo

David Ward, Nashville, Tenn.
Alan Mooney, N.Y.C.

The Significance of War

Elizabeth Gaither, West Edmeston, N.Y.

Coping with Stardom—ANTHONY DEXTER

Jane Hoffman, N.Y.C.

Happiness is the Right Hat—S. I. HAYAKAWA

Rosemary Gilbert, Cincinnati, Ohio

Down and Out in Paris and London—J. PAUL GETTY

Scott Charles, N.Y.C.

A Dictionary of Three-Letter Words—STEPHEN SONDHEIM

Marilyn Rubin, N.Y.C.

Pompeii and Herculaneum Yellow Pages

Ann Brown, N.Y.C.

Cheerleading Greats

> Joan Mintz, Beltsville, Md.

Tax Loopholes for the Middle Income Group

> Lois C. Barth, Staten Island, N.Y.

Single Entendres—MAE WEST

> Joyce Spetrino, Cleveland Heights, Ohio

A Cultural Guide to Las Vegas

> Bill Jackson, Piermont, N.Y.

Diary of a Lilliputian

> Susan Fishman, N.Y.C.

Fat Is Beautiful

> Estelle Strongin, Brooklyn, N.Y.

My Secret Life—NED ROREM

> Roger Freudigman, N.Y.C.

☞ Double Dactyls

Higgledy Piggledy
Romeo Montague,
Thought his love dead and so
Poisoned himself.

Juliet, hasty but
Eschatological,
Died lest she leave him a-
Lone on the shelf.

Above, a double dactyl. Competitors were invited to submit their attempts at this form of verse.*

Report: Roosevelt, Humperdinck,/Calcium Cyclamate,/ Beethoven, Bonaparte,/Seemed to repeat./ Cassidy, Kennedy (Aristotelian); Some, like the centipede,/Too many feet.

---

* Rules for this verse form are contained in the excellent collection: *Jiggery Pokery: A Compendium of Double Dactyls,* edited by Anthony Hecht and John Hollander, drawings by Milton Glaser. Atheneum.

Higgledy Piggledy
Yale University
Gave up misogyny
Opened its door.

Coeducational
Extracurricular
Heterosexual
Fun is in store.

Fred Rodell, New Haven, Conn.

Higgledy Piggledy
Abraham Eisenberg's
Driving a taxi with
Duty light on.

I say: "To Harlem." With
Instantaneity
I'm on the pavement and
Eisenberg's gone.

David Axlerod, N.Y.C.

Grumpily, lumpily
Ursus horribilis
Stomps through the woods on his
Plantigrade feet;

Haunched rather hugely, tailed
Rudimentarily;
Both breath and temper are
Not very sweet.

Katherine Parkes, N.Y.C.

Higgledy Piggledy
Tom Tom the Piper's Son
Purloined a porker and
Forthwith he fled.

Passersby said this was
Incomprehensible
Due to the yarmulke
Worn on his head.

William McGuirk, South Toms River, N.J.

Higgledy Piggledy
Jacqueline (Kennedy)
Tossed a photographer
Over her head.

Changing his countenance
Melodramatically:
Curious (yellow) to
Furious (red).

Peter Hochstein, N.Y.C.

Higgledy Piggledy
Hadrian, Pontifex,
Swished through the Vatican,
Puffing his fag;

Said, "Mother's feeling her
Infallibility
In this delicious pon-
Tifical drag."

Robert A. Day, N.Y.C.

Higgledy Piggledy
Oedipus Tyrannos
Murdered his father, used
Mama for sex.

This mad debauch, not so
Incomprehensibly,
Left poor Jocasta and
Oedipus Wrecks.

Joan Munkacsi, N.Y.C.

Higgledy Piggledy
Thomas A. Edison
Gave us the light bulb
To use in dark spots.

Now power companies
Illuminatedly
Charge us for using their
Heaven-knows-watts.

Robert H. McGovern, Columbus, Ohio

Hickory Dickory
Simon and Garfunkel
Think girls like Rosemary
Something sublime.

Old Mrs. Robinson
Superseductively
Tried to make Art but he
Didn't have thyme.

Debbie Beller, Brooklyn, N.Y.

Hawkery Pokery
Baltimore Orioles
Soared to the stadium
Hungry for Mets.

Strange are the destinies
Ornithological!
Proudest of birds became
Turkey croquettes.

Douglas Scott, Brooklyn, N.Y.

Higgledy Piggledy
Beverly Silverman
Checking her billing had
Only one gripe.

So she corrected it
Nomdeplumerrily:
SILLS can be printed in
Much bigger type.

Roger Sturtevant, N.Y.C.

Misericordia!
College of Cardinals,
Nervously rising to
Whisper its will:

"Rather than being so
Unecumenical,
Can't we just quietly
Swallow The Pill?"

James Lipton, N.Y.C.

Higgledy Piggledy
Samson the Nazarite
Said to a hippie with
Hair past his ears:

"Watch what you're doing, O
Ultrapiliferous,
Don't pick a girlfriend who's
Quick with the shears."

Mary Catherine O'Connor, Convent, N.J.

Rat-a-tat Rat-a-tat
Edward G. Robinson,
Gangsters and killers are
Your cup of tea.

I concede you're the best
Galvanizationist
If I should doze off while
Watching TV.

Dale Roop, Bayside, N.Y.

Higgledy Piggledy
Good ex-Saint Christopher
Strolls through the golden streets
Feeling no pain.

Though he no longer is
Hagiographical,
Speeders can't worry him
Ever again!

Msgr. A.V. McLees, St. Albans, N.Y.

Shubada Shubadee
Cannonball Adderley
Came on the scene like a
Bolt from the blues.

His popularity
Coincidentally
Left me more leisure for
Romance and booze.

Paul Desmond, N.Y.C.

Higgledy Piggledy
Marion Morrison's
Sissified moniker
Gave him a pain.

Transformed by Hollywood
Cinematography,
Now he is famous as
Tough-guy John Wayne.

Florine McCain, N.Y.C.

Higgledy Piggledy
Baron von Frankenstein,
"Don't you get lonely?" "Well,
Sir, that depends:

"Through my experiments
Sociomedical,
I've found a marvelous
Way to make friends!"

Peter Haas, N.Y.C.

Hippity Hoppity
Hopalong Cassidy
Hopped on old Topper and
Brought down the horse.

Since then old Hoppy has
Lopped off some weight—what with
Polyunsaturates,
Walks, and remorse.

Roy Blount, Jr., Brooklyn, N.Y.

Tiffety Taffety
Madame de Pompadour
Loved *crème brûlée,* such ex-
Pansive desserts.

After developing
Steatopygia,
She was the one who in-
Vented hoop skirts.

Emily Barnhart, Pittsburgh, Pa.

Higgledy Piggledy
Richard the Lion-Heart,
Locked in his tower, made
Piteous moans.

Passersby, hearing him,
Unhesitatingly
Called out, "That's terrible—
Bring on the Stones!"

John and Susan Peters, Staten Island, N.Y.

Higgledy Piggledy
Theodore Roosevelt
Looked at San Juan and cried
"Charge!" to each man.

Would you believe that this
Pseudohistorical
Shout was the start of the
Master Charge Plan?

Norman Storer, White Plains, N.Y.

Higgledy Piggledy
Stephanie Quackenbush
Met a young student when
Going to lunch.

Matters progressed so that
Etymologically
Stephanie shortened her
Last name to Wunsh.

Mrs. Stephanie Wunsh, Pittsburgh, Pa.

Higgledy Piggledy
Nicholas Romanov
Started the domino
Theory, 'tis said.

Not being much of a
Parliamentarian
Tsar of all Russias was
Soon in the Red.

Jane M. Gullong, N.Y.C.

Fiddledee Faddledee
Alice in Wonderland,
First she was tiny and
Then she was tall,

Argued with animals
Anthropomorphical,
Didn't accept their con-
Clusions at all.

Willard R. Espy, N.Y.C.

Higgledy Piggledy
Harold M. Hollingsworth,
Known to the world as a
Scholar of note,

Spends his odd evenings
(Pseudoprofessional)
Writing this verse which he
Hopes you will quote.

Harold M. Hollingsworth, Dallas, Texas

Missable, kissable
Judas Iscariot:
Mary B. Gallagher
Followed your lead.

Your reputation in
Numismatology,
Next to her profits, seems
Paltry indeed.

Nancy Andrews, Rosemary Rothschild, N.Y.C.

Higgledy Piggledy
Ivan the Terrible
Brought to his bedroom a
Girl in her teens.

Later she said to this
Sexagenarian,
"So that's what 'Ivan the
Terrible' means."

Linda Arnswalder, N.Y.C.

Higgledy Piggledy
Liam O'Flaherty
Touring Iran, stopped to
Visit the Shah,

Praising his host and his
Beautiful country, said
Unpatriotically
"Erin go blah."

Neil Isaacs, Knoxville, Tenn.

Flibberty Gibberty
Catherine de Medici,
Luxury loving and
Keen for romance,

Headed for Paris and
Connubiality;
Wound up the mother of
Three kings of France.

Elizabeth Pierce, N.Y.C.

Higgledy Piggledy
C. Northcote Parkinson
Said, "Work expands to fill
All of the time."

Here at my desk I find,
Characteristically,
Dactyls expand to fill
All of the rhyme.

Mrs. Paul Lippman, N.Y.C.

Higgledy Piggledy
Ivan the Terrible,
Tsar of all Russia, feared
Treasonous darts.

Eagerly using his
Cinematography,
Eisenstein captured him
Filmed in two parts.

William Thut, N.Y.C.

Higgledy Piggledy
Father James Kavanaugh
Looks at his church which seems
Quite out of date,

Needing revision in
Extraterrestrial
Bothersome matters of
Conscience and fate.

Ann Levin, Newtown, Pa.

Hurkimy Lurkimy
Anton van Leeuwenhoek,
Grinding his spectacles,
Found they were strange,

Thought he'd originate
Microbiology,
Which he invented by
Changing the range.

S. Maguire, N.Y.C.

Do re mi, Do re mi
Ludwig van Beethoven
Hardly could guess when he
First hummed the song

It could express such an
Un-German sentiment:
Cryptogrammatically
(short, short, short, long)

Joseph Wisnovsky, N.Y.C.

Higgledy Piggledy
Hopalong Cassidy
Rode our TV sets each
Saturday night.

His scripts were naïve and
Unpsychological
Bad guys wore black hats and
Good guys wore white.

Marcia and Jack Sanders, Brooklyn, N.Y.

☞ *Kitty Foyle*

Well-born folk specializing in breeding of London policemen: BOBBIE GENTRY
One who sends Vikings by Parcel Post: NORMAN MAILER
Gambit by clever mouse: KITTY FOYLE

Above, three excerpts from our *Dictionary of Fractured Names*. Competitors were invited to submit definitions for well-known persons.

Repeats: TAB HUNTER: a thirsty dieter; NOEL COWARD: a Scrooge; HARRY REASONER: hirsute logician; GROUCHO MARX: frown lines or poor grades; JUNE HAVOC: college commencement; MICKEY MANTLE: disguise for spiked drinks; DINAH SHORE: what you do when not eating aboard ship, also, a prehistoric animal; TUESDAY WELD: construction workers' memo following "Monday, Rivet"; W. C. FIELDS: a portable outdoor loo; JOHNNY CASH: for pay washrooms.

Merciful wrestling hold in which no strain whatsoever may be brought to bear: PORTIA NELSON

One who drives parrots to a complete mental breakdown: POLLY ADLER

Rees Behrendt, N.Y.C.

A builder of executive washrooms for the Navy: CAPTAIN JOHN SMITH

A private nook for reading Longfellow: EVANGELINE BOOTH

Alfred D. Berger, N.Y.C.

A guy who puts his goddam car wherever the hell he pleases: FRANK PARKER

Campbell's Annual Report: SOUPY SALES

Toni Evins Marks, N.Y.C.

A scholarship fund for postmen: CARY GRANT

Long hard pole fashioned by cavemen from plants for use in war: BASIL RATHBONE

Neil S. Meltzer, Flushing, N.Y.

Superb cook having a meal: EYDIE GORME

Dating Bureau statistic: ELLA FITZGERALD

Gordon Peavy, East Hampton, N.Y.

Lament of African pygmy after fruitless day spent hunting elephants: SPIRO AGNEW

Terse reply of Jacob when asked by Rachel what he calleth their youngest begotten: JOE NAMATH

Harry V. Lugauer, Milwaukee, Wis.

A French Alpine dog who gets sick in wet earth: BERNARD MALAMUD

Mrs. Edith Felber, Westbury, N.Y.

Species of acrobatic Italian louse: HEDDA HOPPER

Virtuoso on the efremzimbal: EFREM ZIMBALIST

Dan Greenburg, N.Y.C.

A pilot's reply to radio tower's description of runway:
ROGER MUDD

Joan Wosahla, Ridgefield, Conn.

What Mrs. Claus said when asked where her husband's tabby was: NICHOLAS KATZENBACH

Tom Hunter, N.Y.C.

An addict of a particular brand of cigarettes: MUSTAFA KEMAL

Farmer's reply to wife when asked about egg production in hen house: SOMERSET MAUGHAM

Michael R. Verona, N.Y.C.

Question asked by Brooklynite wanting to know what's wrong with Hoover's FBI: SAMANTHA EGGAR

Wanda P. Halsey, N.Y.C.

Dilemma faced by martini drinkers: OLIVER TWIST

John Kallir, Scarsdale, N.Y.
Ann Brown, N.Y.C.

A homosexual prayer shawl: GAY TALESE

Swishy pedestrian: NANCY WALKER

Jerome Lawrence, Malibu, Calif.

Signal from one McCoy to another McCoy when a "hit" is scheduled: MARK HATFIELD

Sophia Orr, N.Y.C.

What I go to the dentiss for: MATISSE

The great French derailment: TOULOUSE-LAUTREC

Leonard Zimmerman, Brooklyn, N.Y.

Announcing the Emperor (Josephine couldn't make it):
NAPOLEON SOLO

> *William Perlmuth, N.Y.C.*

Room with bath: JOHN LODGE

> *Betty O'Hara, Los Angeles, Calif.*

A Jewish general's Christmas song: DIAHANN CARROLL

A tepid Florida out-island: KEYE LUKE

> *Martin Charnin, N.Y.C.*

Just the whites, please: YOKO ONO

> *Barbara Schein, White Plains, N.Y.*

A Latin who murders for jewelry: RUBY KEELER

In praise of French dessert: CHARLOTTE RAE

> *Esteban Chalbaud, N.Y.C.*

Quotations from William the Conqueror: NORMAN WIS-
DOM

A district in the London derrière: FANNY WARD

> *Walter Shea, Mount Vernon, N.Y.*

Time of day one feels most lonely: MISCHA AUER

> *Steve Tuttle, N.Y.C.*

Free sample cigarettes: WINSTON GUEST

> *Theodore Cordes, Hollywood, Calif.*

Award for Best Documentary Film on Animal Life:
OSCAR WILDE

> *Robert P. Schron, N.Y.C.*
> *Christie Kennard, Shawnee Mission, Kansas*

A giant white rabbit in the Marines: HARVEY KORMAN

> *Stuart Bochner, West Islip, N. Y.*

A transvestite: TOM TRYON

> *Michael Calandra, N.Y.C.*

Multileveled bathrooms for Members of Congress: SENA-
TOR JOHN TOWER

> *D. Frischer, Kansas City, Mo.*

RCA preferred stock: VICTOR MATURE

> *Nora Greenburg, N.Y.C.*

An effete radio with absentee father and dominant
mother: FAYE EMERSON

> *Alan Rachins, N.Y.C.*

Boss of the prison newspaper: CON ED

> *Robert Sekuler, Evanston, Ill.*

Fashionable Irish brawls: DONNY BROOKS

> *Charles Hollerith, Jr., N.Y.C.*

An exploding cigar: MURIEL SPARK

> *Michel Merle, Institute, W. Va.*

Bathroom tissue salesman on Fire Island: MARY, QUEEN
OF SCOTS

> *Chris Zingg, N.Y.C.*

A cockney corset: FANNY BRICE

> *Diana Wyngarden, Van Nuys, Calif.*

Ritual suicide performed by convicted perjurers in
Japan: HARRY TRUMAN

> *Martin Israel, N.Y.C.*

One who checks Turkish hats: FESS PARKER

Sign posted throughout The Netherlands for the conven-
ience of tourists: JOHN UPDIKE

> *Judy Clegg, N.Y.C.*

Typical comment of Chinese laundryman to landlord: I.
M. PEI

Idie McGinty, St. Louis, Mo.

Thick stew much enjoyed by German army during World
War II: GERRY MULLIGAN

The officer in charge of seasoning same: HERB SARGENT

William Tynan, N.Y.C.

Le Havre dockman who beats up on smaller guys:
PIERRE BOULEZ

Arthur Rubinstein, N.Y.C.

Import duty imposed on French athletic supporters:
JACQUES LEVY

Marvin Goodman, N.Y.C.

Color the dope red: CARMINE DE SAPIO

Tom Morrow, N.Y.C.

The man Scarlett O'Hara thinks about: TOM MORROW

Arnold Cover, Sarasota, Fla.

Bathroom, carried by tornado to the Emerald City: JOHN
OSBORNE

Tom Kennard, Shawnee Mission, Kansas.

Tyro studying to be an Apostle: PAULA PRENTISS

Francine Siedleki, N.Y.C.

The Paris peace talks: SITTING BULL

Robert Allen Laurent, Lafayette, La.

Ponce wore this after a long drink at the fountain: LEON
BIBB

Bob Kessler, N.Y.C.

Outdoor carpet: SONNY TUFTS

> *Lynda Sunderland, Sunnyside, N.Y.*

Texas power: WELLS, RICH, AND GREENE

> *Les and Iska Fraidstern, N.Y.C.*

Nero: CHRISTIAN HERTER

> *Dwight Dobbins, Peapack, N.J.*

Horse-drawn vehicle for transporting Scottish musicians:
PIPER LAURIE

> *Angelo R. Papa, Trenton, N.J.*

Underground synagogue: EMANUEL CELLER

> *Joe Bigelow, Beverly Hills, Calif.*

Transsexual: BEN HUR

> *Robert Fountaine, Valley Stream, N.Y.*

☞ "Man Was Not Meant to Tamper with the Unknown . . ."

"Man was not meant to tamper with the unknown. . . ."

"You may kill me, Herr Major, but hundreds will rise to take my place, and we'll keep coming until you and your kind are defeated. . . ."

Above, typical final dialogue from, respectively, Horror and World War II movies. Competitors were invited to submit invented last lines for two film categories.

DETECTIVE: "After that final lingering kiss she was gone. I stepped out of the terminal to feel the sun rising over my city—opening another day of excitement, tragedy, and joy—on 42nd Street, my beat."

WORLD WAR II: "Joe, I'm finished—listen—she's yours, Joe—kiss her for me and tell her uh . . ."

Roy N. H. Larsen, Old Tappan, N.J.

COMPOSER BIOGRAPHY: "It will come to you, Hansel, I know it will. I can hear it now, in the Kunstplatz. Dum dum ta dum. You will be immortal, Hansel, and, perhaps, they will remember me, too."

JAPANESE P.O.W. CAMP ESCAPE: "Well, not quite all present and accounted for, Colonel. There was Mario, and Bernie, and Lieutenant Lowell Cabot Adams, the Harvard guy, but the rest of us made it, sir, one way or another."

Elaine Kendall, Princeton, N.J.

THIRTIES ROMANCE: "Say, lissen, ya big swell-headed palooka, a girl would hafta be cleah outa huh mind to put in with a bozo like y— hey! put me down, ya big ape. Aw, gee, Bill honey, but I'm nuts aboutcha. . . ."

SCI-FI: "Yes, Earth is safe again, but still . . . I can't help feeling that those things wanted to be our friends. . . ."

Herbert Hartig, N.Y.C.

BRITISH WAR ROOM: "Oh, yes, chaps, one final word. If you fail, as I'm sure you all now know, all is lost. That's it. Good luck . . . and good hunting."

AMERICAN NEWSPAPER OR COURTROOM OR MEDICAL EPIC: "I think I'd like that drink now."

Brian Vachon, N.Y.C.

SOUTH SEAS: "Husband Steve has come back to his Mamua. Heart of Mamua once more sing like goona bird."

PRIVATE EYE: "It was his limp that tipped me off. A man shot in his right leg doesn't limp with his left. Take my advice, Flanagan, and quit readin' them cheap detective stories."

Michael Deskey, N.Y.C.

ROONEY-GARLAND MUSICAL: "Guess what, Judy! Rotten Nick McKee confessed he's the one who stole Miss Blankenship's life savings, and he's in jail, and your brother's been released, the bank's going to lend us the money to remodel the old barn, and guess who's out there in the audience, having the time of his life—Flo Ziegfeld! So, *places everybody, for the finale!*"

Max Wilk, Westport, Conn.

JUNGLE: "Jane, Boy, look at Cheetah. Ha ha ha ha ha ha ha ha ha."

WESTERN: "He pulled out this mornin' pret' near 'bout as quiet as he come, and I reckon he'll never know just how much good he done this town."

Warren Burton, N.Y.C.

GANGSTER: "I'm top dog, do you understand? Top dog! The king of the world, that's me! Nobody puts anything over on Johnny Angel!" (*Dies*)

SOCIAL DRAMA: "They hounded us—and tried to destroy us, Cassie. But we're too strong for them. We're . . . the *people!*"

Ted Sennett, Closter, N.J.

SCI-FI: "Your cobalt-uranium missile has done it, professor. The creature is dying."—THE END ? ? ?

WESTERN: "Now you're the fastest gun, Kid. And somewhere there's a young gunman waiting to test you."

Miles Klein, Belle Harbor, N.Y.

FIFTIES SCI-FI: "Perhaps now, we, as creatures of this new world, can avoid the old pitfalls of fear and mistrust and build a life based upon peace and unity as *He* originally ordained."—THE BEGINNING

FORTIES COMEDY-MYSTERY: "Ya know, kid, I think you and me have a lot of catchin' up to do."

Stephen D. Mackler, Orange, N.J.

DETECTIVE: "Well, there's your cat burglar, Miss Judy, so how's about you and me going somewhere to celebrate?"

THRILLER: "You're right, doctor, I should never have called it a 'silly native superstition.' "

Henry Morgan, N.Y.C.

NOBLE HORSE: "She won! She won, Gramps! Star Lad Won! We can *keep* the farm. . . ."

Ed Schultz, N.Y.C.

DISNEY-TYPE NATURE: "The newborn fawn trembles her way to the gently sloping banks of the pond, dips her head in, drinks her fill. . . . Another day on Pawhawk Pond has begun. And so the circle closes once more . . . life . . . death . . . and life."

Martin Gross, N.Y.C.

COSTUME EPIC: "After him, you fools. Forty thousand dragos for his head!"

Gary Gladstone, N.Y.C.

HOLMES-TYPE WHODUNNIT: "But only the pawnbroker had seen Armbruster enter the Turkish bath. It couldn't have been Penelope because she's allergic to animal dander. And the midget spoke no Hindi. By the simple process of elimination, that left only the meteorologist and Swanson. Need I remind you of the weather conditions on the night of the crime?"

Norton Bramesco, N.Y.C.

HOLMES-TYPE WHODUNNIT: "Yes, he had it all worked out: the fake trip to Mozambique, the news of the fatal surfing accident, then the insurance and the wife. He was the streetcar conductor, you know, and the spurious ballerina and the cannibal witch doctor as well. Fiendishly clever, but for what, Dustbin, for what?"

Michael F. Lipp, Bogota, N.J.

SCI-FI: "Don't cry, Timmy, the giant mollusk wasn't really happy in the big city."

Howard Pasternak, Brooklyn, N.Y.

JOAN CRAWFORD: "Love? You ridiculous fool. Don't you understand? We *used* each other. And there's nothing left. Nothing!"

Patricia Miller, N.Y.C.

FIGHT: "Sure, the young punks laughed at him, and maybe he should have quit years ago, but he had a heart as big as all outdoors and we'll never see his like again. He'll always be the *champ.*"

David Yarnell, N.Y.C.

SPORTS: "Thanks, Lord—that's one I owe you."

Charles Rubin, Rye, N.Y.

SOPHISTICATED N.Y. COMEDY-MYSTERY: Southern Girl (to Nora and Nick on street corner): "Pardon me, can y'all tell me how ah can get to the zoo?" (Nora and Nick look at each other remembering how it all began, and run off screaming, "Oh, no!") ". . . Well, ah do declare!"

Marvin Aledort, N.Y.C.

WORLD WAR II: "The story you have just seen, and the characters in it, are fictional. But acts of courage like these are occurring day after day, in Europe and the Pa-

cific, as American fighting men and women, and those of
our valiant allies . . . without their noble inspiration,
this motion picture would not have been possible. . . ."

Dodi Schultz, N.Y.C.

C. CHAN: "Murderer reveal self when Number One Son
pretend to be cow in barn."

Karen Sorensen, N.Y.C.

HORROR: "What a shame he couldn't have turned his
genius to good instead of evil. . . ."

WESTERN: "Well, if you ever change your mind, stranger, this here marshal's star will be waitin' for
you. . . ."

John F. Farley, N.Y.C.

GANGSTER ROMANCE: "We're from two different worlds,
baby. This can't be. Go back to your kind, and I'll go
back to mine. When I see you in the society pages and
you read about me in the police reports, maybe we'll remember when we passed in the night. . . ."

James T. Burns, N.Y.C.

VAMPIRE: "My daughter, God save her, can rest in her
grave—*now.*"

Sidney Shore, N.Y.C.

MELODRAMA: "I always felt you were more than just a
friend . . . *Mother.*"

Rosalie Uffer, Bayside, N.Y.

ORPHAN: "It's time for us to go home now . . . *son.*"

Louis J. Boasi, N.Y.C.

WESTERN (homesteaders versus cattlemen): "Come along, son . . . let's take your mother *home*."

D. Corman, Framingham, Mass.

ARMY TRAINING FILM: "Remember, men, when you protect yourselves, you're protecting your country."

Arthur Penn, Philadelphia, Pa.

SUPERNATURAL: "The ghost is happy that we know who she is, and so we will live here in peace and never hear from her again."

Beatrice Jaraslow, East Northport, N.Y.

ANDY HARDY: "Well, son, I'm sure we've all learned a great deal about honesty and the human heart from this experience. . . ."

DR. KILDARE: "Well, son, I'm sure we've all learned a great deal about honesty and the human heart from this experience. . . ."

Rosemary Bascome, Shelter Island, N.Y.

JR. H.S. GUIDANCE: ". . . so remember, even though there are forty ways to brush your hair properly, only Mom and your family physician and you can choose the best way for you."

Rosalie Guzofsky, Glendale, N.Y.
P. Spivak, Detroit, Mich.

TEEN ROCK EPIC: ". . . You know, Martha, maybe these kids have the right idea after all. . . ."

S. Feldman, Roslyn Heights, N.Y.

WORLD WAR II: "Take a last look down there and say good-by, to that godforsaken jungle."

Bob Erxleben, Des Moines, Iowa

COWBOY: "We were sure wrong about you, mister. You can really handle that gun."

Anne Commire, N.Y.C.

SCIENTIST: "The fools, fools! As if destroying my equipment and burning my house down can stifle the boldness of the human imagination. . . ."

Jack Paul, Brooklyn, N.Y.

WORLD WAR II: "I can't go back to England with you, Scotty, but I'll be seeing you when the lights go on again, all over the world."

Annalee Gold, N.Y.C.

WESTERN: "The banditos, they weel be eating bread an' water for a long time, Ceesko, but you an' me, we weel eat tortillas tonight, no? Ho, ho, ho . . ."

Suzanne Frankle, Youngstown, Ohio

BOXING DRAMA: "Hey, Duke, listen to this in the *Chronicle*: 'Last night Billy (the Kid) Jackson won the world's lightweight crown. . . . Metro City hasn't seen such a display of fisticuffs since Duke Jackson,' . . . that's you, Duke. . . . 'A few old-timers know that Duke, who lost his sight after that bout, trying for the crown, runs a newsstand somewhere in the city. But how many know that Billy Jackson is Duke's kid brother and that when Duke went blind he vowed to stay out of the kid's life, never to reveal who he was until the kid won the crown? So the kid won more than the crown last night. He won a long-lost brother. . . .' "

Marvin Goodman, N.Y.C.

☞ *"Lie Down with Apes . . ."*

"Lie down with apes, and you get up with apes."
"Death is life's answer to the question 'why?'"
"A superfluous cat is less than no cat at all."

Above, some meaningless proverbs for all occasions. Competitors were invited to submit equally pointless adages.

"The hairless sheep has few admirers."

"The stars do not wait until the king's birthday to shine."

"A white cake may have chocolate frosting."

"You don't have to break your leg if someone gives you a crutch."

"A short man on horseback can look down on a tall man on the ground."

"A honking goose is soon spotted."

"The dog who bites you may have his reasons."

James E. Ricketson, N.Y.C.

"Beware of the man who will not brandish a plaster cast of his foot!"—Japanese proverb in Haiku

"O! For a two-handled broom!"—Cambodian

"Even a doctor can laugh!"—Yiddish

"It is better to wear out your slippers dancing than to have your feet cut off."—Russian

"An Eye for a Tooth."—Transylvanian

"Rain before seven, dark by midnight."—Cape Cod, U.S.A.

"If a man is hungry, then he will eat."—Polish

Hermine Stover, Brooklyn, N.Y.

"Consider the mouse before he considers you."

"A man must remove his shoes before you can judge his socks."

"Remember, the Princess phone has been there and back again."

"A fool has no business inside a balloon."

Herb Sargent, N.Y.C.

Some Russian Proverbs:

"He who drinks borsht with a cross bear may carry home salt, but he will limp."

"Only a fool walks to Minsk on a Tuesday."

"While three wise men can pull a troika, a fool can be eating kasha."

"He who harvests at Easter will find pigs in his bed."

"If only rich men could have ugly daughters the Czar would be a woodcutter."

Sanford Zane Meschkow, Woodside, N.Y.

"If God wanted us to go to concerts He would have given us tickets."

Jason Farrow, Boston, Mass.

"I met a man with a hearing aid. Then I met one who didn't know how to peel an apple."

Norton J. Bramesco, N.Y.C.

"There are only three things that are sure in life: Marshmallow, plum pudding, orangutans, and chairs."

Edward Rothstein, N.Y.C.

"It's a poor secret that has no agent."

Mrs. James A. Roy, Honolulu, Hawaii

"The fact that monkeys have hands should give us pause."

R.D. Malloy, Brooklyn, N.Y.

"Fool me once shame on you, fool me twice shame on you, fool me three times shame on you, fool me . . ."

Helene Kaplan, N.Y.C.

"A true buffalo never turns its head to the wind."

George S. Lowman, Chicago, Ill.

"A wet bird never flies at night."

K. Lever, Greenwich, Conn.

"Little things come in small packages."

Mrs. Emile Renan, N.Y.C.
Irwin and Roberta Berger, N.Y.C.

"He who neither drinks, smokes, nor eats hay is not fit company for man or beast."

Rosemary Smith, Caldwell, N.J.
Nancy Borriello, Fairfield, N.J.

"A bird in hand makes it difficult to blow your nose."

Richard Betten, N.Y.C.

"There is no excuse for poor health."

Elliott Ames, N.Y.C.

"It is far better to sit idle than to just do nothing at all."

Joen Ellen Kanze, North White Plains, N.Y.

"It is better to have a hundred gloves than no hands."

Andrew Aaron, Riverdale, N.Y.

"All work and no play make Maude a dull name."

C. Schuman, N.Y.C.

"A man may be short and fat, but he is usually bald."

David Fractenberg, New Paltz, N.Y.

"You can't straighten a snake by pulling it through a straw."

Martin Charnin, N.Y.C.

"You need never be alone if somebody is with you."

Martin E. Healy, Bronx, N.Y.

"Give a dog a bad name—and he'll like it as well as Fido."

Lili Krakowski, N.Y.C.

"A Rolling Stone gathers Groupies."

Edward J. Butler, N.Y.C.

"A strange bedfellow is better than none."

Alfred D. Berger, N.Y.C.

"There is no gift like the present."

Mark Scheinbaum, N.Y.C.

"The dumb man asks no questions of his deaf wife."

Shan Ellentuck, Roosevelt, N.J.

"More than fish escape the man who fishes in a fishless sea."

Alan Kraus, St. Louis, Mo.

"In the restaurant of life, it's a foolish diner who fails to tip his Captain."

Dan Greenburg, N.Y.C.

"Frank Necessity is a Mother of Invention."

Aristides Pappidas, N.Y.C.

"The fruits of mankind are footprints in the snow of oblivion."

Craig Johnson, Winnetka, Ill.

"A thirsty man has nothing for tears."

Baird Searles, N.Y.C.

"You can always go back, but you can never return."

Marilyn Rubin, N.Y.C.

"A man for all seasons can ice skate sometimes."

Art and Eileen Boyle, Lakewood, N.J.

"He who casts no shadow knows no shame."

Mrs. Paul Lippman, N.Y.C.

"Strife is a runcible spoon."

J. Elizabeth Wykoff, Keyport, N.J.

"Rise to the occasion, and the occasion will surely come up."

Catherine Youngling, Boston, Mass.

"The grass is greener after it has been painted."

Thomas F. Schweitzer, Queens Village, N.Y.

"Old goats make good wineskins."

John N. Gish, Jr., Hackensack, N.J.

"Not every firstborn becomes king."

Samuel M. Hudson VII, Cambridge, Mass.

"Why work if you can carry your lunch?"

Brien E. Bednare, M.D., Englewood, N.J.

"Never shake hands with a stricken cat."

Mark Greitzer, N.Y.C.

"Size is no mark of a little mind."

Barbara T. Williamson, N.Y.C.

"A faithful woman gathers no fur."

Judith O'Donnell, Staten Island, N.Y.

"To roll a cheese uphill, one must first conspire with the mosses."

Mrs. R.W. Sawicki, N.Y.C.

"Good music fades into the past, good books into the future."

Stu Schrank, Albany, N.Y.

"Lost causes rest in narrow beds."

Arthur S. Nislick, Huntington, N.Y.

"The hand that turns the doorknob opens the door."

D. H. Anderson, Fort Lee, N.J.

"Artificial fruits have no pits."

Marc D. Levitt, Brooklyn, N.Y.

"You can make a pigskin wallet out of a sow's ear."

Arno H. Scheiding, Darien, Conn.

"Though the night be long and stormy, she's still your mother."

J. Herbert Silverman, Dobbs Ferry, N.Y.

"In numbers there is quantity."

Richard Connolly, Lake Hopatcong, N.J.

☞ *Keir Dullea, Gone Tomorrow*

Keir Dullea, gone tomorrow
Menu item: Pâté, Maison, and La Verne

Above, the phrase is familiar, but the name is cant. Competitors were invited to submit familiar phrases involving punned versions of well-known names.

Repeats: Absence makes the heart grow Fonda; a Stritch in time; Albee a monkey's uncle; the friendly skies of Unitas; Barrymore not on the lone prairie; Hello, Dali; Picasso You; Miri Miro on the wall; a fool and his Monet; Molière than thou; neither Abe Burrows nor a lender be; *honi soit qui* Lily Pons; I love my wife, but oh, Euclid; Tarzan Stripes Forever; Descartes before the horse; beauty in the eye of the Bill Holden; U Thant take it with you; old soldiers . . . just Faye Dunaway; Nixon stones will break my bones; The Agnew and the Ecstasy; monkey see, Pompidou.

In hoc Señor Wences

Haim Ginott now, nor have I ever been a member of . . .

It Marcus Welby spring

> *M. Brim, J. Livingston, Cambridge, Mass.*

Menu:
Chicken Alan King, Wild Risë Stevens
Hearts of Artie Shaw/Rockefeller Dressing

> *Carol Brener, N.Y.C.*

Anne Klein Nacht Musik

There's a little Iphigenia in Aulis

Judith H. Crist, what a dump!

> *Tom Lacy, N.Y.C.*

Jeanne Crain Corn and I Don't Care

Helen Hayes no fury like a woman scorned*

Ina Claire Day You Can See Forever

> *W. Baker, M. Flanagan, West Lafayette, Ind.*
> ** M. K. Blohm, South Hadley, Mass.*

My heart tells me this is Rudolf Bing

You Ain't Ben Blue

It's a Long Way to Tex McCrary

> *Neil D. Isaacs, Knoxville, Tenn.*

On a Keir Dullea You Can See Forever

> *Lois C. Fein, Brooklyn, N.Y.*
> *Tita Curtis, N.Y.C.*

Here today, Guatemala

> *Harold Marshall, Mamaroneck, N.Y.*

The Bert Lahr did it

Wee Wendell Willkie

> *Mrs. Jane Herron, St. Louis, Mo.*

When you care enough to send Nathanael West

Mrs. Edward Powell, Jr., N.Y.C.

Maddox and Englishmen go out in the midday sun

Sharon C. Fodor, Greens Farms, Conn.
S. and H. Wallach, Roslyn Heights, N.Y.

Nabokov in a carload

J.W. Crolly, Savannah, Ga.

The Best Years of Burl Ives

Ade Kahn, N.Y.C.

But soft, what light in Rhonda Fleming breaks?

Burton Miller, Los Angeles, Calif.

King Kong the Witch Is Dead

Bill Hicks, Brooklyn, N.Y.
William Harris III, Los Angeles, Calif.

Who was Scott Brady I saw you with last night?

Susan Trainor, Astoria, N.Y.

Little Miss Muffet sat on a tuffet, eating her Curtis LeMay

Diane Fajen, Jackson Heights, N.Y.

Yvonne DeCarloan?

Ruth Tauriello, N.Y.C.

Row, row, row your boat gently down the stream,
Merrill Lynch, Pierce, Fenner and Smith . . .

R. and A. Herz, N.Y.C.

Patachou, Patachou, baker's man

Donald B. Malm, Beverly Hills, Calif.

We were sailing along, on Turhan Bey

Bob Barry, N.Y.C.

Lafayette, Vuillard here!

James F. O'Connor, N.Y.C.

Wait Attila the Hun Shines, Nellie

Mrs. B. Hoffman, Monterey Park, Calif.

I'd like to get you on a slow Botticelli

Mrs. M. De Vries, Morristown, N.J.

Raymond Burr the Alamo

Fay Bainter or for worse

Mrs. Richard West, Cheverly, Md.

Flow Janet Leigh, Sweet Afton

Harris Sarney, Brooklyn, N.Y.

Honi soit qui Mollie Parnis*

Anna May Wong, but I Think You're Marvelous

Michael Davenport, Union City, N.J.
* Evelyn Greene, Great Neck, N.Y.
* Richard Fithian, N.Y.C.

Willa Cather at the River

Rees Behrendt, N.Y.C.

Alice Faye in love and war*

What this country needs is a good five Saint Subber

Joan M. Kelleher, New Rochelle, N.Y.
* Lenn Curley, San Francisco, Calif.

Getting Goethe's Garter

Michael Deskey, N.Y.C.

Why, man, he doth bestride the narrow world like an Onassis

Christopher Ausschnitt, Philadelphia, Pa.

Ira Levin, incompetent and immaterial

> *Barbara Ringer, Washington, D.C.*

To be Arnold Toynbee, that is the question

> *Theodosios Athas, N.Y.C.*
> *Hope Raymond, N.Y.C.*
> *J. Cavett, Pacific Palisades, Calif.*

Godzilla Acre

> *Ronnie Allan, Highland Park, N.J.*

Hocus-pocus Lainie Kazan

> *Larry Boram, Pendleton, Ind.*

You Know Ida Cantor Hear You When the Water's Running

> *Henry Wohl, N.Y.C.*

Ali MacGraw is divided in three parts

> *Daniel J. Moriarty, N.Y.C.*

Ruby Dee dub, three men in a tub

Karajan, Nurse

> *James Fechheimer, Glen Head, N.Y.*

The Alan Jones connected to the Jack Jones, the Jack Jones connected to the Tom Jones, the Tom Jones connected to the Dean Jones . . .

> *Frank Jacobs, N.Y.C.*

Coriolanus, you're the answer to a prayer

> *Bill Tourin, N.Y.C.*

Yankee Doodle went to London Michelangelo Antonioni

> *A. Harris, Valley Stream, N.Y.*

Stuck a feather in his hat and called it Mickey Rooney

E. Kark, Parama, Ohio
A.G. Miller, N.Y.C.

Zapata of little feet

Telephone Message: Simon, call Peter

Marilyn Cirrone, Staten Island, N.Y.

Regis Toomey, I can't find my glasses

Gibbs Murray, N.Y.C.

John Wayne on My Parade

Joe Masteroff, N.Y.C.

I am not my Brothers Karamazov

Donald Wigal, N.Y.C.

Stone walls do not Fred Brisson make

Pauline Kline, Brooklyn, N.Y.

Metro Golda Meir

Carol Pavsner, Southfield, Mich.

You are old, Father William, Henny Youngman said

M. Berlin, N.Y.C.

L'Amour Toots Shor L'Amour

Mary Chesnut, Chappaqua, N.Y.

In the beginning Dodd Mead heaven and earth
Life Is Chester Bowles of Cherries

Albert G. Miller, N.Y.C.

Liza Minnelli with soul so dead, who never to herself has said

Mrs. Robert Amft, Evanston, Ill.

Thou canst lead a horse to Walter Matthau canst not make him drink

Ethel Strainchamps, N.Y.C.

Sardi's child must work for a living

Fred Rodell, Bethany, Conn.

Damn the torpedoes, full Edith Head!

I know a little bit about a lotta things, but Antonioni 'nuff about you

N. and E. Hufford, N.Y.C.

I Vonnegut married

Mrs. F. Van Poznak, Ridgefield, Conn.

Footloose and Frances Dee

Janet Harris, Levittown, N.Y.

Brother, Agnew Spiro dime?

Stanley Green, Brooklyn, N.Y.

High on a Wendy Hiller

Thomas Costner, N.Y.C.

Menu Item: Goldilocks and Bagels

Arnold Soboloff, N.Y.C.

Kunstler at Law

David Yarnell, N.Y.C.

A Tale of Thucydides

Harold Stone, N.Y.C.

I've Grown Augustine to Her Face

Michael Olmert, Annapolis, Md.

I Don Juan to set the world on fire

Mrs. Paul Stein, N.Y.C.

I lost my keys, how am I Gunga Din?

Karl Levett, N.Y.C.

ReJoyce Brothers the best is yet to come

Harriet Rosenblum, Pittsford, N.Y.

And, of course:
Bennett Cerf than sorry

Helen Bayler, Brooklyn, N.Y.

Mike Dolby, the Hero of Our Tale

Mike Dolby, the hero of our tale, was a virtuoso on the accordion, but otherwise had few interests.

Above, the first sentence of a novel we never finished reading. Competitors were invited to submit a similarly uninviting opening sentence of a novel destined for oblivion.

"You won't believe the size of the bug I just killed up in Gregor's room, dear."

Arthur Penn, Philadelphia, Pa.

Jane W. Williamson, age sixty-three and divorced, was a roomer-boarder-lodger with the Arthur Rivers family on April 1, 1970.

Kathleen K. Scott, St. Paul, Minn.

In the late spring of 1933 (just ten years after my arrival on this earth), my father, the president of a small-town bank in the Midwest and a great believer in FDR, startled my mother during lunch with an announcement which none of us realized at the time would certainly color our lives dramatically in the decade to come.

Styrk Orwoll, Cincinnati, Ohio

"Who was it said, *Errare est humanum?*" Darley asked, with a faint smile, as he poured her another martini.

JoAnn West, Cheverly, Md.

The border war between the two Eastern European duchies had persisted for decades, but it did not stop Lizalotta and Itzak from continuing their Sunday picnics of black bread and currant jam near the customs shed.

Paul Noble, N.Y.C.

When Baylor Condon's huge arm drove his subtle hammer ringing against the seasoned anvil (*prenez garde!*) the surfeit gorged (*toujours perdrix*) townspeople gathered at their windows in awe at the one man, their *terrae filius,* who had brought Mark Dorman, *gentilhomme,* to Clintsburg and made it overnight into the malacology capital of Zenith County.

E. B. Markus, San Diego, Calif.

The tale I am about to unfold took place in an unnamed country in an unnamed era, and I will call the characters "the man" and "the woman."

William Cole, N.Y.C.

She was the best of sex, she was the worst of sex, she was at the age of wisdom, she was at the age of foolishness, she was the epoch of relief, she was the epoch of turmoil, she was the spring of hope, she was the winter of despair, she was everything for me, she was too much for me, she could send me directly to heaven, she could send me directly the other way—in short, she was so much like other girls . . .

Michael Donovan, N.Y.C.

It was the best of times and the worst of times in our happy family—unlike any other happy family—and I wanted to grow up stately, plump to be the middleweight boxing champion of Princeton and the hero of my own life . . . incidentally, call me Ishmael.

Malcolm Braly, N.Y.C.

Call me John Galt; who is Ishmael?

Wilma Miller, Merrick, N.Y.

Call me Izzy.

E. Bernstein, Brooklyn, N.Y.

Call me a *schlemiel*.

E. M. Thompson, N.Y.C.

As the sun slowly sank into the great Pacific, he flang his surfboard onto his brawny shoulder and made his way up the beach through admiring female gazes.

Joseph A. Pollard, Downey, Calif.

An international movie star at eighteen, I must debunk the myth of "overnight" success: it was a long agonizing struggle that began six months ago when this producer . . .

Jack Paul, Brooklyn, N.Y.

He walked back to the motel in the rain.

William Michaels, Devon, Pa.

Mycroft P. Mapes sat in his posh mid-town public relations office and let the fingers of his mind sift lovingly through details of the previous day on which his client, a short Bronx lawyer of Italian extraction, had been elected mayor of New York City.

Norton J. Bramesco, N.Y.C.

Pasquale Dorio was a happy man: at last, at last he had located enough stones to build fencing around all four sides of the world, and his heart leaped joyfully as he urged his burro toward Isabella's castle—surely she would help him!

Mrs. Edward W. Powell, Jr., N.Y.C.

Ktath, the Gomaq of the Cliff People, stared out into the pale sunlight and scratched his pelt.

Richard Steinfeld, Houston, Texas

"The biggest tease in town!" was the way the men who met in Sam's Barber Emporium described Mabel Hunnicutt's "Sunday get-together" at "Mab-Roy," the big white house on the hill.

Jim McFairline, N.Y.C.

Buffie and Bounce were finally off with Aunt Muff to their long-awaited holiday on Crag's Moor.

Tom Morrow, N.Y.C.

Ondine, Ultra Violet, and Taylor Mead all thought I should call this second novel "B."

Robert J. Cahn, N.Y.C.

It had been a bad year for selling secondhand sewing-machine parts, and no one knew it better than John Fogle.

Michael Sage, N.Y.C.

Honkee Ratt, leader of the midget wift cretins from the planet Zurn, turned to his ferocious blue pig, Randall, and said, "Attack!"

Judith P. Harris, Philadelphia, Pa.

It was a dark and stormy night.

Patricia Samson, Cedar Falls, Iowa

For what must have been the fiftieth time, the intrepid Collins turned over in his mind all the details of the twenty-year annuity he proposed to sell to Goodrich.

Arnold Rosenfeld, Dayton, Ohio

Janice threw her soft-boiled egg at the new Rauschenberg hanging in the breakfast nook, and screamed, "I don't want *art*, you fool, I want *you!*"

Paula Drechsler, Palisades, N.Y.

Rain was falling on the city, drip, drop, drip, drop.

Joe Masteroff, N.Y.C.

"Reginald, fetch me my slippers from the drawing room," said Smith thoughtfully.

Ed Hooks, N.Y.C.

Wills Jones was half-Chinese; he had tried to make it as a boxer.

Rosemary J. Ford, Washington, D.C.

At first glance, it was obvious that Peggy Perky was affected by cosmetic—rather than cosmic—influences.

Mrs. Dorothy Kaufman, N.Y.C.

The laird of the manor had the gout and there was a singular lack of levity at the mansion; Penelope had spent the morning tutoring the children and now had returned to her chambers to work on her needlepoint.

Michael Deskey, N.Y.C.

Morty Prisson was not happy with the wording on page 13, article 51, paragraph 3, line 6 of his new total coverage insurance policy.

Mary Wright, N.Y.C.

It was on our 450th orbit of Mars that Commander Bullit began to look at me with a peculiar, burning intensity.

Suzanne Wochos, Washington, D.C.

After forty-five years in slag, Edward Brunk finally believed he knew the business.

Peter Spivak, Detroit, Mich.

John was a peasant boy who had a way with poultry.

Bill Sklar, Bethlehem, Pa.

The toothpaste was running out of the tube now, which meant that I had to put the cap back on each morning.

Mrs. Vincent Conroy, Astoria, N.Y.

Bombo, dog of the North, howled mournfully down the vast wastes of the Tundra . . .

T. V. Gubler, Coopersburg, Pa.

"Ah, my dear Ivan Nikolayevitch, allow me to present Lizavet Alexandrovna and Vladimir Pavlovitch."

Ellen S. Ryp, N.Y.C.

Having lost now, oh, forty-odd *New York Magazine* competitions, he calmly went to the drawer, removed the pistol, and placed the muzzle to his head.

A. and J. Spielberger, N.Y.C.

Nick Adamson, Senior Assistant Vice-President of *Fly-By-Night Radar* made his groggy way to the refrigerator, chose three ripe V-8s for his morning juice, glanced at Mary Lou Cohen's column in the local newspaper long enough to see that next week's meeting of the Clairvoyants' Society had been canceled due to unforeseen circumstances, and meticulously sauntered his six-foot two-hundred-pound Herculean body over to the pantry to awaken his devoted Dalmatian, Spot, and his voluptuous new wife, Rita.

Jared Weinberger, Morristown, N.J.

"I liked being a virgin better," she said.

Frances A. Lebowitz, N.Y.C.

"Where can my dumb boyfriend be?" she thought as she walked to her pink Princess telephone.

Ad Orkin III, Jackson, Miss.

Being blind did not keep me from hearing the squeak of little Tommy's wheel chair or the crackling crescendo of the approaching flames.

Donald Wigal, N.Y.C.

Opening her locker with one hand and fondling the ring around her neck with the other, Maryanne felt proud to be Vito's girl.

Minette Siegel, Los Angeles, Calif.

As I take my pen in hand, dear reader, I am ever mindful of my wife's gentle insistence that it is my obligation as a novelist (dare I call myself that name?) to guard against letting his mind wander.

David M. Boehm, N.Y.C.

☞ *Outside, Somewhere, a Dog Was Barking*

He started to leave, then he turned and went back to her; outside, somewhere, a dog was barking.

Above, the final line of an uninspired work of fiction. Competitors were invited to submit the last line from a bad novel.

Leaning against the stone statue, he closed his eyes for he felt tired; then he poured the last of the champagne into her mug and suddenly it was going to be all right.

Frank O'Connor, Omaha, Nebr.

Mike Dolby had never felt so tired and, as his head slowly slumped forward in his easy chair, the pages of his unfinished accordion concerto dropped from his hand waking Forepaws at the hearth; "No need to worry," thought the dog, his master was only sleeping.

Michael Deskey, N.Y.C.

I thought of all the ways I could have answered her; I thought of the farmyard stoop where we had played as innocent children; I thought of her voice, caressing yet incisive; I thought of her arms, embracing yet supply muscular; I thought of the way her body moved as we strode the traplines on the short winter mornings; I thought of the long winter nights we had spent together in our log cabin beside the banks of the Susquatch hard by the headwaters of the great Nahanni; I thought of love and I thought of love betrayed, and I turned on my one good heel and limped out of her life for ever.

David Cobb, Toronto, Canada

The leaves are falling again; perhaps it is Evelyn under that distant umbrella, perhaps not.

Charles Almon, Brooklyn, N.Y.

". . . Catch her, you fool," but the voice was drowned in the sturdy-gurdy of life as that absurd monkey, Chance, with one and two left feet danced his desperate jig while her soft, broken heart lay gasping on the ground.

Kate Cox, N.Y.C.

. . . the tears, he told himself, were from the wind.

Tony Chiu, N.Y.C.

Lit up brightly by the fulgent pulsing light emanating from the death-dealing volcano, like stroboscopic lights on a cheap dancer in a modern night club, or like flashes of brilliance from a worthless genius, Maralee brushed her shining auburn hair back with her hand, and smiled.

Linda C. Franklin, N.Y.C.

Beneath her chartreuse scales, tentacled limbs, and piercing, lidless eyes, Fwmka of the fourth planet was a person, too—he knew that now as he stared, unseeing, at the slowly clotting iridescent pool on the floor of the cell.

Dodi Schultz, N.Y.C.

She began to depart, then she turned back and went to him; outside, somewhere, a cat was meowing.

Alan Kaltman, Highland Park, N.J.

The dog started to leave, then he turned back and went to the bitch; outside, somewhere, a man was calling.

Allen Glasser, Brooklyn, N.Y.

"I'm the President now, ain't I?" he said in his flat, toneless voice, and before anyone could stop him they watched in horror as he slammed his ham-like fist down on the red button that was to end everything for everybody—everywhere.

Stanley Gilson, N.Y.C.

". . . But," thought Barney as he huddled through the cold rain heading uptown, as the chief had said, "she was . . . no girl for a cop."

Tom Morrow, N.Y.C.

Thus was Simon de Grasse created Duke of Arwerk, King Louis's kingdom strengthened, Count Agnst reunited with his daughter, the Bishop of Ome elevated to Cardinal, the town of Luce saved from the Huns, Alain and Margarite wed, the University saved from financial ruin, the cathedral of Tyre rebuilt, Lord Quentin punished, Robert de Fontaine restored to his ancestral home, the power of the dread Lindsley crushed. Lady Montaigne delivered of twins, and little Brett made joyous again.

Joel Frome Crystal, Brooklyn, N.Y.

He darted up the four flights as effortlessly as an Olympic sprinter, threw open the kick-pocked door marked 4B, and shouted into the disheveled room, "Selma, I'm home! I'm home!"

Robert Lasson, Newton, Mass.

Jenkins took my cap and muddy fatigue coat, smiled for what must have been the first time in his life, and said, "Welcome back to Three Oaks, Master Jimmy."

Barry Orton, New Brunswick, N.J.

As the white stallion mounted a small rise opposite the corral, he paused and looked back, and Peter understood for the first time why he couldn't follow him; as the tears formed he felt Uncle Hank's big hand rest lightly on his shoulder.

James A. Todhunter, Staten Island, N.Y.

I knew, as did Lot's wife, not to turn back . . . but like Lot's wife, I was human too.

Bonnie Schwartz, N.Y.C.

Lying near the torn thing that had been Sir Arthur Jervis was the fabulous jade idol—the curse of Pfthoth had been fulfilled!

Robert E. Goode, N.Y.C.

There was only a moment left for years of remembering —she blew him a kiss and took one last look . . . behind his glasses, his eyes were missing.

Eugene Stone, Palo Alto, Calif.

"My God, Thelma, she's been dead for seven years" . . . "Eight, Martin—eight."

Monte Barer, North Bergen, N.J.

For a moment time stood still as the bullet with his number on it pierced that great big heart and silenced it forever.

Jerry J. Cole, White Plains, N.Y.

"Igor will do the trapeze act in the center ring; Buck would have wanted it that way."

Michael Goldberger, Hewlett Harbor, N.Y.

There was a tea bag in the Margarita.

Marcia Tallmer, N.Y.C.

Seeing the Star glistening in the cold sky outside the barn, the boy fell to his knees beside the newborn colt; "Hello, Little Christmas," he said tenderly. "Welcome to the Bar-7 Ranch."

Albert G. Miller, N.Y.C.

"Miss Nellie? Oh no, sir," cried the old woman, "she's not here, she took the morning train for Toronto."

Catherine Lahart, East Northport, N.Y.

Nigel knew what he must do.

William Cole, N.Y.C.

"Your wife called, sir," Witherspoon told the inspector, "said something about burned bridges."

Hedley M. Burrell, Washington, D.C.

It was as if that cricket in the back of his mind had rubbed its legs too long, too furiously, and was silent—forever.

Howard B. Means, Washington, D.C.

"Why," he puzzled, "is the catcher the victim of the catch?" as he caught the raindrop in his eye and moved blindly down the street.

C. Richard Williams, N.Y.C.

"How much better," he thought, the rays of the rising sun prismed in his tears, "if we had trusted Man and not Men."

Warren Randall, Levittown, N.Y.

As he stood in the wings waiting to go on again after those long years, wondering if it could ever be the same, the orchestra struck up his theme, the applause started, and he knew that whatever else happened in his life, this is where he belonged.

Marvin Goodman, N.Y.C.

He knew, somehow, that he would never return to this rock, never wear these shoes again, never see Laura; he turned and walked, his back to the sea, until he was lost from sight among the bracken.

David Axlerod, N.Y.C.

As soft and as light as flamingo, she fairly danced down the long curving staircase, catching glimpses of herself as she went in the mirror that followed her white satined image and flattered her pale shoulders until the perfumed magnolias enveloped her as she waltzed onto the veranda and into a dazzling display of cascading pink and white roses gently framing the cake and she closed her eyes tightly and whispered a silent prayer.

Lynne C. Gillen, Philadelphia, Pa.

He stood at the crossroad for a long time, staring at the wagon path that led through the red desert to Navajo country and his people; he thought of Little Dancer in the Rain and knew she was out there too, waiting. Suddenly he turned, jumped into the Bugatti, gunned it, and roared down the highway to L.A.; he never looked back.

Phillip Bloom, N.Y.C.

It was a cold and rainy night in March; off in the distance a hoot owl screeched her plaintive cry, while in the darkened front room of the big house, a newborn child greeted the world with lusty infantile indignation.

Nancy R. Finn, N.Y.C.

She opened the door a crack, then hesitated, closing it quickly, while fumbling to hastily remove hair net and curlers; the broken pane of glass had been replaced.

Elsie N. Bradley, Hackensack, N.J.

One last surging memory of his model as she had been in life skyrocketed through his consciousness; then, as the slim brush, still heady with its heavy oils, slipped through his gnarled stained fingers and plinked to the floor, Jason whispered, "Estella . . . my darling, at least *this* way you'll live forever!" . . . and was gone.

Nathalie Grant, New Orleans, La.

Margaret sat rigid, immobile, her eyes blind to Martin's departing form, her ears deaf to the softly closing door, her cheek oblivious to the fly which tarried there absorbed in its own ablutions, mindlessly (oh, fortunate creature!) stropping one foreleg upon the other like some grotesque medieval armorer; and when the first tear finally fell, he too, his honing done, had already taken flight.

David E. Diener, Irvington, N.Y.

And she, her eyes a silent storm, saw through it all, and stayed for more.

Carey B. Gold, N.Y.C.

The phone rang four times, was silent, then rang again and I knew who was trying to reach me but I let it ring.

Mrs. Eileen King, Washington, D.C.

And there in the faded elegance of the hospital garden, she greeted Dirk on Sunday afternoon, her dark eyes now purged of their luminous ferocity, the tapering fingers of her murderess's hands now docile in her lap; the specter of what-might-have-been hovering between them.

Mrs. Hilary Beckett, N.Y.C.

"Harrow Hall belongs to the National Trust now, and they tell me that the old dungeon is now a discothèque, called, appropriately enough, Maiden's Peril."

Elaine Kendall, Princeton, N.J.

As he stood on the edge of the cliff, he still heard her screams and saw the trusting smile on her face that she left behind, burning forever in his mind's eye.

Patricia Kerman, N.Y.C.

Maybe it was because he lived at a time in the world's history when the beautiful seemed obscene and the obscene was a thing of beauty.

A. Greene, N.Y.C.

Home . . . home . . . Derek started running . . . not caring . . . dropping his belongings as he rushed forward . . . his coat, the tattered suitcase . . . his past.

Lee Bailey, N.Y.C.

The sloop, a dead thing now, creaked and groaned painfully in its death throes.

Armand Stella, Ridgewood, N.J.

She picked up the only untrampled rose from the floor, brought it gently to her face in her cupped hands, and with a whimper the tears came, "My God! It's plastic too!"

Jan Wunderman, N.Y.C.

Years later, a boy and girl walking through the old cemetery at twilight told of seeing a man who resembled the infamous "Trigger" Collins place a rose before the old tombstone that read simply "Susan Wilcox—Her Only Fault Was Loving Me."

Gloria Lichtenstein, Bayside, N.Y.

It was the same face, the same smile, and I said to myself, "Well, here we go again."

Jerald Silverman, Pearl River, N.Y.

She knew now that life upon the wicked stage was nothing for a girl, but she also knew that she was a woman and David Galasco was holding auditions tomorrow for *Sin Sweep City*—David Galasco!

Charles Love, N.Y.C.

Now Melulu understood and a light went on in her heart; she was a girl, and Captain Olsen was a boy.

Patricia Miller, N.Y.C.

The children knew that at last the mystery had been solved: "Sleep soundly, Bridget Wentworth," said Ellen.

Richard Feinbloom, N.Y.C.

"So this is what it's like," he thought, as the water closed over his head.

Gridley Fidel, Brooklyn, N.Y.

"Steerage won't be so bad," he thought.

Herb Sargent, N.Y.C.

Don Roderigo de los Fuentes y Velasques smiled as he straightened his peruke; "I think we will see no more of the Blue Tarantula."

Norton Bramesco, N.Y.C.

And they did.

Mrs. Leona Ozols, Mount Kisco, N.Y.

. . . which is another story.

Sam Bassin, Brooklyn, N.Y.

☞ *Shampoo: an Impostor Bear*

SHAMPOO: an impostor bear
MESCALINE: sloppy Irish girl

Above, excerpts from our fractured dictionary. Competitors were invited to submit similar definitions for words starting with the letters A and B.

Repeats: ADAMANT: the first insect; ANTACID: his LSD; ARCADE: Noah's beverage; BROCADE: welfare; ADVERSITY: Madison Avenue; ALLEGRO: rockettes; APHRODITE: infant dashiki; BORDELLO: laconic greeting; BOUDOIR: peace rally; BEFUDDLE: football conference; ACQUIRE: chorus; BOMBARD: bad poet; BARBARIAN: topless waitress; BACCHANAL: Venetian alley; BACHELOR: folk tales; BENEDICTION: drug habit; BANSHEE: stag party; AWKWARD: bird sanctuary; BRANDISH: cereal bowl; ALGEBRA: mermaid's undergarment; BUCCANEER: overpriced corn; ACOUSTIC: pool implement; ABALONE: nonsense!; BOLOGNA: maxi-dress; ALKALINE: baseball player; ALLOCATE and BIFURCATE: Miss Hepburn, hail and farewell.

ARTERIOSCLEROSIS: noted orchestra conductor of Greek-Italian descent who was chronically late for concerts at

Carnegie Hall due to heavy crosstown traffic; hence, any-one so afflicted

BUGABOO: primitive means of banishing insects by sneaking up behind them and frightening them to death; seldom effective

Dan Greenburg, N.Y.C.

ANTELOPE: the secretive marriage of two consenting in-sects

BISECT: the process by which anteloped couples divorce

Judy Knaize, N.Y.C.

ASPERSION: Iranian beast of burden

BALUSTRADE: dance given by Sherlock Holmes for Scot-land Yard official

Byron E. Fox, N.Y.C.

AUREOMYCIN: small furry rodents which thrive on cookies with hot pink centers

BANISTER: British attorney for anti-bomb groups

D. Kotteb, N.Y.C.

AFORE: popular and much-in-demand room at the Hotel Dixie, N.Y.C.

BENIGN: unpopular and always-vacant room at the Hotel Dixie, N.Y.C.

Karen Issaacs, N.Y.C.

ABBEY: dear

BLOSSOM: dearie

Betsy Gehman, Middletown, Conn.

ACERBITY: a small knight

Mrs. John Rorke, Summit, N.J.

BOOMERANG: last prize in pie contest
Marvin Aledort, N.Y.C.

BUMPKIN: unpleasant Mafia assignment
Price Walker, N.Y.C.

BRONTOSAURUS: treasury of works by nineteenth-century English sibling authoresses
Mrs. Paul Stein, N.Y.C.

BROADCAST: the players in a Clare Boothe play of the 1930s
E. Harrison, Brooklyn, N.Y.

BOULDERS: a hard rock group
Laurie Barrow, N.Y.C.

BAYONET: a small girl from a town near Newark
R. E. Feinberg, N.Y.C.

BLEMISH: the official language of Felgium
Robert W. Rossi, Rochester, N.Y.

ANTIDISESTABLISHMENTARIAN: question addressed by A. Hitler to elderly Munich hostess
James Fanning, Mount Kisco, N.Y.

BAS-RELIEF: guest critic for John Simon's column
Arnold Cover, Sarasota, Fla.

AMBERGRIS: slightly darker than biege gris
Frank Walker, N.Y.C.

ATTRITION: an ignored President's daughter
Nancy Bernard, Los Angeles, Calif.

BLANCMANGE: a disease of the scalp exclusive to blondes
Ronald Bohn, Los Angeles, Calif.

ANASTOMOSIS: what God gave in order to transport the tablets of the Ten Commandments down Mount Sinai

Louis Heifetz, Somerville, Mass.

BASICNESS: craving to leave San Francisco

Loren Lomansky, Hartford, Conn.

APOSTLE: a package from the Bronx

BAROQUE: can't pay for Apostle

Burns Copeland, Waldwick, N.J.

BIDET: D-Day minus two

Albert G. Miller, N.Y.C.

BARCAROLE: Liliom (Billy Bigelow)

Dan Rodden, Andalusia, Pa.

BIRACIAL: how Jacob begat

Bill Goldschlag, Fort Lauderdale, Fla.

BALLYHOO: what island did you say?

Hyman Levy, N.Y.C.

BACCALAUREATE: where Will Rogers stood

Ellen Kattelle, Brooklyn, N.Y.

AROMA: focal point, all roads

Dale McAdoo, N.Y.C.

ANNUNCIATION: recruitment of Sister of Charity for intelligence work

James F. O'Connor, Arlington, Va.

ABNEGATE: entrance to Dogpatch

Susan Ressler, N.Y.C.

APPARENT: member of the lost generation

BALDERDASH: what Yul Brynner has

Bel Kaufman, N.Y.C.

AUTOEROTIC: drive-in movie

Trudy Drucker, Newark, N.J.

BUNION: bialy

Mrs. Arthur Michaels, N.Y.C.

BROUHAHA: the joy of cooking

J. B. Hapgood, Quogue, N.Y.

BOMBAZINE: a very bad weekly (in England, a very good weekly)

Rosemarie Heyer, N.Y.C.

BADINAGE: woman of forty celebrating her twenty-ninth birthday

Nancy Kessler, Bayside, N.Y.

BETTING: a highly popular activity not well regarded in some circles; e.g., big boliceman interfere with people they find betting

Barry and Arlene Klingman, Santurce, Puerto Rico

ABATTOIR: third man up for the Paris Bombers

Carol Topilow, Bronx, N.Y.

BAGEL: Massachusetts tern

Betty Forman, New Haven, Conn.

ANTEDILUVIAN: one who is against the support of Paris museums

Marvin Goodman, N.Y.C.

ACIDIC: sentence often found in children's readers

Patricia Dowd, Flushing, N.Y.

BAMBINO: expression used by a mother deer when reprimanding offspring

Susie Kranz, N.Y.C.

BICENTENNIAL: sexually confused one-hundred-year-old

Paula Drechsler, Palisades, N.Y.

ASTRONAUT: what the Apollo XIII mission accomplished

Mrs. Barbara Rich, New Rochelle, N.Y.

BUFFET: a gay shoeshine boy

Hilary Solomon, White Plains, N.Y.

ACIDULATE: Southern U.S. expression repeating accusation of tardiness

Mrs. Robert Saulnier, Easton, Conn.

ALOOF: top of a Chinese house

Alan Burke, N.Y.C.

BANDAGE: American epoch, circa 1940

Ruth S. Cage, N.Y.C.

ASCORBIC: painful brand-name ballpoint pen

Steve Goldmacher, Brooklyn, N.Y.

BELFRY: 1. a call without message units 2. AT&T after the revolution

Paula Weideger, N.Y.C.

ALABASTER: his wife's not nice, either

Lola Fuir, N.Y.C.

BARBEQUE: little girls in a toy shop

Robert Andrews, Green Bay, Wis.

APPENDAGE: before typewriters

Sally Walworth, Plainfield, N.J.

BOUILLABAISSE: Yaleman's kiss

Eunice Weed, N.Y.C.

BLINKS: a Japanese armored-car service

Marshall W. Karp, N.Y.C.

ACTIVATE: Abbie Hoffman, *et al.*

Vivian Nash, New Haven, Conn.

ABUNDANCE: a hot cross fox trot

Arthur J. Cunningham, N.Y.C.

BRUISE: sad music on the Ginza

Norton Bramesco, N.Y.C.

ANTIPASTO: weight-watchers

Bernard H. Cohen, M.D., N.Y.C.
Mary Costa, Brooklyn, N.Y.

BISEXUAL: a Southern prostitute's greeting

Charlotte Curtis, N.Y.C.

APOLOGIST: short summary of moon shot

Mary Scott Welch, N.Y.C.

ANNIHILATION: euphoric feeling around the Pentagon

Joseph T. Rigo, N.Y.C.

BIGAMY: a large, small person

William Honig, N.Y.C.

ARROGANT: a shirt company merger

> *Robert A. Clark, Cincinnati, Ohio*

ALTERCATION: Evangeline in drag

> *Bob Henabery, N.Y.C.*

BRANDY: loser in toothpaste competition

> *Allan B. Smith, N.Y.C.*

ABDOMINAL: a kind of snowman

> *L. D. Burg, New Cumberland, Pa.*

AUSTERE: *Myth.* British animal, 'arf-'oss, 'arf-steer

> *Eileen Hall, Tarrytown, N.Y.*

BITUMINOUS: purchase a couple of out-of-date dresses

> *Suzanne Suskin, Kansas City, Mo.*

BUNKUM: grooming aid for rabbit's hair

> *Ruth A. Spear, N.Y.C.*

BACILLUS: *Myth.* Roman god of germs

> *Carol Drew, Palisades Park, N.J.*

BACTERIA: the chic private club behind every Horn & Hardart's

> *Tom Morrow, N.Y.C.*

BENIGN: what you can't wait to do when you're eight

> *Jeffrey Rich, New Rochelle, N.Y.*

ABBREVIATE: the cheese we had yesterday

> *Hank Levinson, N.Y.C.*

ASYMMETRICAL: derrière-reducing diet drink

> *Ellen Sweeney, N.Y.C.*

ARITHMETIC: a thucthessful doctor

> *David G. Miller, N.Y.C.*

BLUNDERBUSS: a baby carriage

> *Michael Deskey, N.Y.C.*

BEATNIK: Santa on December 26th

> *Paul J. Brinson, Kenmore, N.Y.*

BAILIWICK: air freshener with South Seas sandalwood

> *Carol Diamond, N.Y.C.*

BELLICOSE: a shave by a Chinese barber

> *Marvin Safir, N.Y.C.*

BUSHWHACK: female Australian soldier

> *Tom Bahring, Fort Holabird, Md.*

APOCALYPTIC: four bushels of cosmetics

> *Hal David Brown, Ballwin, Mo.*

AEROSOL: El Al pilot

> *L. Harvey Levine, Manhasset, N.Y.*

ATTENDANCE: a five-couple prom

> *Brenda Gustin, N.Y.C.*

AUDITORY: a British accountant

> *Albert Rubin, Woodhaven, N.Y.*

ALTERNATIVE: a person born during the wedding cere-
mony

> *Roy Blount, Jr., Brooklyn, N.Y.*

BILIOUS: in debt

> *David R. Scott, Princeton, N.J.*

AMNESTY: the way I react on nasty days

Joan Weiss, N.Y.C.

AXILLARY: to question Sir Edmund

J. H. Burke, N.Y.C.

ANCILLARY: what to do when questioned by Mr. Spivak on *Meet the Press*

Robert F. Dean, Raleigh, N.C.

☞ *Richard Nixon and the Vice President Are on Safari . . .*

Richard Nixon and the Vice President are on safari. A herd of animals thunders past and one animal comes between the two men. Thus, Spiro Agnew is for a moment, *a hartebeest away from the President. See?*

Above, a far-fetched fable. Competitors were invited to devise a brief story including and clarifying any punned or otherwise mangled aphorism.

Smetana mistakenly showed up at a theater across the street from the one in which his opera was playing. He didn't know which side his bride was bartered on.

Henry Morgan, N.Y.C.

"Listen, Nanook baby, sign with me and I'll make you a star. No more documentaries, igloos, seals, and blubber. It'll be musicals, girls, fun, and laughs. Just stick with me, kid. Flaherty will get you nowhere."

Robert Weissberg, Old Tappan, N.J.

Johann Sebastian was gettin' on in years when a neighbor's child asked for a piggyback ride. "Carry me, Bach." "Too old, Virginny."

Henry Wohl, N.Y.C.

When the maharaja forbade the killing of tigers, and the populace, its safety jeopardized, rose up and deposed him; it was reign called on account of game.

George Stoddard, Mendham, N.J.

At the Stratford-on-Avon kindergarten, young Will Shakespeare meets Lester, whose father, Mr. Greeck, is of Latin descent. "Mommy," Will reports at home, "I know a small Latin, Les Greeck."

Hubert B. Herring, N.Y.C.

The main event is an aborigine tag-team match: the wrestlers are natives tonight.

A. Barry Levine, N.Y.C.

The little baby cannibal wouldn't eat his dinner. "What's wrong with leftovers?" asked the mother cannibal. "Nothing" answered the baby. "I just feel like a new person."

M. Fidel, Brooklyn, N.Y.

When *New York Magazine* picked a safari as location for the Competition example, its choice was an *Afroism*.

Mimi Weisbond, N.Y.C.

The admiral loves books. But not the best seller about how to stop the Navy from stifling officers. So, if you want to give the admiral a gift, don't give *Up the Ship*.

Donald Wigal, N.Y.C.

A policeman, seeing Leo Durocher, runs to get his autograph. But he loses sight of Leo when he walks behind a clothesline filled with girls' underwear. . . . Verily, there's many a slip twixt the cop and the Lip.

Albert G. Miller, N.Y.C.

And so, by order of Premier Meir, the Canal was reopened; and in order to make defense of the waterway easier, the area was defoliated. To this day it is known as Golda Locks and the Bare Trees.

Burns Copeland, Waldwick, N.J.

An expedition uncovers Captain Kidd's treasure, but, until more men can be sent, it is hidden in an apiary owned by an aged man and his son. The following message is sent to the base camp: "Booty is in the beehives of the older."

Idan Simowitz, Laurelton, N.Y.

The old sheep clipper was aching from a particularly heavy work load. The next day, still unable to work but wanting to complete his wool collections, he sent his young assistant, the sore shearer's apprentice.

Mrs. Paula Van Brink, N.Y.C.

The owner of the N.Y. National League baseball club is named an honorary member of the team by its manager. But the players find it hard to think of her as their peer. After all, one man's Met is another man's Payson.

Norton Bramesco, N.Y.C.

Two germs swimming in the bloodstream of a stallion accidentally entered the lymphatic system, where they were devoured by a phagocyte. Moral: never change streams in the middle of a horse.

Mary Lou Durham, Indianapolis, Ind.

Jack was determined to win the *New York Magazine* Competition, but he was only a runner-up. The reason he couldn't concentrate on writing his entry was that this big rabbit (a drinking friend) kept breathing down his neck. You might say Jack missed first prize by a hare's breath.

Jack Rose, N.Y.C.

Senator and Mrs. Russell Long are driving through Japan. At an intersection, the signal is turning red and they are forced to stop. Two Longs don't make a light.

Raanan Smelin, New Rochelle, N.Y.

Eurydice stared at her watch as Orpheus descended toward her. "I've been here three hours waiting for you," she fumed. "Where in Hell have you been?"

Marvin Goodman, N.Y.C.

At the Owens-Corning plant in upstate New York, a family of tiny green frogs lived happily in some long Pyrex tubes stored behind the factory. They were unfortunately asphyxiated when the tubes were packaged, proving that peepers who live in glass hoses shouldn't trust Owens.

R. S. Scott, Rector, Pa.

William Randolph Hearst was riding through Brooklyn on his pet aardvark when someone called out, "Hey, man, who are you?" W.R. replied, "I'm Hearst, with my own pet aardvark."

Wallace Litwin, N.Y.C.

Springtime! Huntley and Brinkley are creating headgear to be worn by Huntley's little girl in a school play. David decides to decorate same with artificial fruit and says: "Let's berry the hat, Chet."

Lorraine Pistilli, N.Y.C.

When accusing Peter Roget of snubbing them in the street, his Quaker friends said: "But, Roget, thee saw us."

Amanda Lovell, N.Y.C.

In the 1920s, a group of jazz musicians got together for sessions to honor their hero, a character in a Scott Fitzgerald novel. They were very talented and were known as the Gatsby Jammers.

Rich Hartman, Schenectady, N.Y.

Brother Herbert was barred from any further work in the monastery's herb garden. He always mistook the dill for the weed.

Jane Otten, Washington, D.C.

Chief Sitting Bull aspired all his life to see his children rise in Indian mercantile society. But, alas, he died never seeing his red sons in the sales set.

Sheldon Spitz, Brooklyn, N.Y.

Before leaving Spain, Pablo Picasso showed his early works in Granada where everyone made fun of them. By ignoring their criticism, he proved that it was but a sneer Andalusian.

Dr. Stephen Yohalem, N.Y.C.

Patrick Aloysius Boyle keeps losing custodial jobs as fast as he gets them, because, you see, poor Pat can't keep from drinking while on duty, and, as everybody knows, a potted Boyle never watches.

Herbert Hartig, N.Y.C.

After the catastrophic earthquake in San Francisco, people regularly paid visits to the huge chasm it created and threw in pennies in order to be generous to a fault.

Barbara Mehlman, Flushing, N.Y.

East Indian adage: Do Not Enter Water Where Guru in Exile Hath Bathed, or don't wade in a punished swami's river.

Garry S. Boross, Nanuet, N.Y.

A Mayan Indian priest asked a local youth, "What God you like? You like Moon?" The boy answered, "No, I like farther, like Sun."

Noel T. Adams, Summit, N.J.

At Mercy Hospital in Melbourne, patients convalesce by drinking a brew named for a local bear. One patient complained of its lumpiness and was told by the attending nun that the koala tea of Mercy is not strained.

C. Moscowitz, Highland Park, N.J.

In the closing seconds of the Super Bowl game, fleet-footed quarterback Joe Upharsin decides to run with the ball. Immediately, the entire opposing team piles on top of him, preventing a touchdown. Thus, this headline on the sports page: "Many Many Tackle Upharsin."

Carole G. Goldberg, Vernon, Conn.

Mayor Lindsay, while strolling in the garden of the mayoral manse, hears the cries of a drowning man from the nearby East River. He attempts to save the man but is stopped by a security officer. As the drowning man sinks, the mayor remarks, "There, but for the Gracie guard, go I."

Stan Freeman, N.Y.C.

As the arrow whisked the apple from his head, the intrepid lad pressed his stop watch. What he did was time Will Tell.

Connie Cooper, Macon, Ga.

Report in small-town newspaper on Northeast industrial magnate's meeting with business rival: *"New York Mag. Is Seeing Competition."*

Michael Robertson, Syracuse, N.Y.

☞ *Doubting and Lowell Thomas*

Doubting and Lowell Thomas
Five Cent and Pete Seeger
Personal and Joan Baez
Smart Ass and Erich Maria Remarque

Above, some odd couples. Competitors were invited to submit similarly improbable pairs.

Repeats: Spa and J. P. Getty; La Plume de Ma and U Thant; Brica and Georges Braque; Sincerely and Leon Uris; I Wonder Who's and Henry Kissinger; Habitual and Bert Lahr; Sang and Sigmund Freud; Kissin' and James Gould Cozzens; Brand and Malcolm X; Sand and Pablo Casals; Compost and Uriah Heep; Penny and Mahatma Gandhi; Null and Jon Voight; Rough and Mario Andretti; Gay D and Tom Seaver; Second and e.e. cummings; Mea Maxima and Robert Culp; Tomorrow and Tom Morrow; Rolling Stones and Peter Maas; Multi and Caterine Milinaire; Filthy and Alan Rich; Meat and Eldridge Cleaver; *Honi Soit Qui* and Lily Pons; Ban and Blanche Thebom; Acapulco and Elliott Gould; Home and Henry James; Orange and Franz Schubert; Runny and Margaret Mead; Alte and Joe Cocker; Home and Elaine Stritch; Viet and King Kong; Under A and John

Cheever; Acute and Friedrich Engels; Waxing and Philip
Roth; Poor Man's and Carter Burden; Sacha and Regis
Toomey; Front and Jerry Orbach; Beo and Thomas
Wolfe; Tin Pan and Muhammad Ali; Smoked and Mao
Tse-Tung; Hello and Salvador Dali; Wooden and Mike
Nichols; Finger and Hal Prince; Generation and Nguyen
Giap; Subway and J.R.R. Tolkien; Choo Choo and Mark
Twain; Mule and Cornelia Otis Skinner; Black and Ty-
rone Power; Pounding and Bennett Cerf; Of All and
General de Gaulle; Nervous and Oedipus Rex; Green and
Louis Pasteur; What's and Mme. Nhu; Ham and Senta
Berger; Elastic and Santa Claus; Human and Orson
Bean; Quit and Joseph Stalin; Make Love Not and Ev-
elyn Waugh; I Am Curious and Ben Blue; Deputy and
Omar Sharif; Lindsay and Cardinal Wolsey; Puttin' On
and Lew Ayres; Underground and Eydie Gorme; Chili
Con and Art Carney; *Women's Wear* and James Daly;
Mobile and Oliver Wendell Holmes; Drop and Paul
Anka; Little White and Chou En-lai; Trolley and Debo-
rah Kerr; and, irrepressibly, Christine Jorgensen.

Bob and Carol and Ted and Alice and Michael Ansara

Sorcerer's and Paula Prentiss*

Harry Lorayne, N.Y.C.
* Lyn Rickert, Pittsburgh, Pa.

La Guerre and A. Finney

A Man For All and Paul Cézanne

Identity and Croesus

Candy Joseph, Paterson, N.J.

Closet and Anthony Quinn

Old Oaken and Samuel Beckett

July and George Furth

Vincent Smedley, N.Y.C.

Buck Rogers' Disintegrator and Ronald Reagan

Andrew Meisler, Bronx, N.Y.

Kumquat and Elaine May

Hotsie and Giorgio Tozzi

Milt and Tutankhamen

Jack Rose, N.Y.C.

Glory and Svetlana Alliluyeva

Robert Hudson, Ridgewood, N.J.

I Can't Hear You, I have A Carrot In and Golda Meir

Robert Remez, Waltham, Mass.
Stephanie Wells, N.Y.C.

Kyrie and June Allyson

Accident and Eva Peron

Joan B. Lobis, N.Y.C.

Sic Transit Gloria and Meg Mundy*

Female Wevolutionists, Fwow Away Your and Jacques D'Amboise

Levy Olfson, South Lyme, Conn.
*Daniel F. Tritter, N.Y.C.

Sunday and Eugene Ormandy

Michelin and André Gide

Mrs. E. Boyno, East Orange, N.J.

Could Be and Willard Wirtz

Guy Lom and Brigitte Bardot

Karen Albamonti, N.Y.C.

Sesame and Beatrice Straight

Tippy and Albert Camus

> *Mrs. Stanley Charren, Newton Center, Mass.*

Noble S. and Ruth Roman

> *Carl Pavsner, Southfield, Mich.*

Tops and José Iturbi

> *J. and H. Williams, Arlington, Va.*

I'm Just A Girl Who and Marguerite Cansino

> *Rees Behrendt, N.Y.C.*

The Mahari and Gail Sheehy

> *Stephanie Grunin, Brooklyn, N.Y.*

Why Johnny Can't and Willis Reed

> *Mrs. Ira Lechner, Arlington, Va.*
> *Susan Shenghit, N.Y.C.*

Arrivederci and Sax Rohmer

> *Chuck Suttoni, N.Y.C.*

Hut Sut and Vera Hruba Ralston

> *Mrs. Diana Cooper, Bronx, N.Y.*
> *J. and N. Molyneaux, N.Y.C.*
> *Edward O. Douglas, N.Y.C.*

Brawla Brawla and William Seward

> *Mrs. B. Israel, New Brunswick, N.J.*

Sleepy and Jean Harlow

> *Larry Eisenberg, Flushing, N.Y.*
> *Patricia Q. Stuart, N.Y.C.*

Carpe and Ngo Dinh Diem

> *Mrs. Ira Selsky, N.Y.C.*
> *Sheila Michaels, N.Y.C.*

All This and Ginny Tiu

Show Me The Way To Go and Lord Hume

> *Duncan Steck, N.Y.C.*

Strepto and Bess Myerson

> *Dr. Stephen Yohalem, N.Y.C.*
> *David Maron, Enlewd, N.J.*
> *David Meister, N.Y.C.*

Sentimental and Carl Czerny

Greta and Benjamin Britten

> *Ed De Blasio, N.Y.C.*

Deuter and George Romney

> *Lorraine Passovoy, Chicago, Ill.*

Status and Vittorio de Sica

> *Edward J. McCabe, N.Y.C.*
> *Hal Hackady, N.Y.C.*

The Easter and McGeorge Bundy

> *J. and N. Clokey, Madison, Conn.*

Serving and Señor Wences

> *Joyce McDermott, Bronx, N.Y.*
> *Mrs. Eileen Selsky, N.Y.C.*

Tabula and Julius La Rosa

> *Hillary Garrison, N.Y.C.*

Alma and Zubin Mehta

> *Leonard Sims, N.Y.C.*
> *Gabriel Katzka, N.Y.C.*

Magna Cum and Estée Lauder

Evander Childs and Andrew Heiskell

> *Helen Weiselberg, N.Y.C.*

Do Re Mi Fa Sol La and President Tito

> *Jane del Pino, Jamaica Estates, N.Y.*

Ineverpromisedyoua and Bobby Rosengarden

> *D. Kotteb, N.Y.C.*
> *Billy Neder, Sugar Grove, Pa.*

Outer and Sigmund Spaeth

> *Stan Freeman, N.Y.C.*

Rain, Rain and Dave Garroway

> *Andrea Schamis, Rockville Center, N.Y.*

Auld Lang and Sidney Zion

> *Bob Feinberg, N.Y.C.*

Oily and Stephen Boyd

> *G. Jessen, Wantagh, N.Y.*

A Member Of The Communist Party and Haim Ginott

> *Dr. Stanley Spiegel, N.Y.C.*

Chief and Billie Dove

Memento and Mae Murray

> *J. B. Hapgood, Quogue, N.Y.*

Kitchie and Wellington Koo

> *Karen Hasselriis, Sayville, N.Y.*

Worldly and Andrew Wyeth

> *Dodi Schultz, N.Y.C.*

Stage Door and Leon Janney

> *A. and R. Herz, N.Y.C.*

One Of and William Du Bois

> *Louis Sabin, Milltown, N.J.*
> *Bernard Lacy, N.Y.C.*

Thou Swell, Thou and Dame May Whitty

Steve Tuttle, N.Y.C.

Moonlight and Frank Sinatra

Jeanne Serruys, Staten Island, N.Y.

Sing and John Millington Synge

Morton Raban, Detroit, Mich.
Joanna Steichen, N.Y.C.

Trompe and Myrna Loy

Barbara Muccio, N.Y.C.

Religious and Edna Ferber

Dale Anderson, N.Y.C.

Veni, Vidi and Leonardo da Vinci

Barbara Smolansky, N.Y.C.
Gisella Baumann, Astoria, N.Y.

One Upman and Dick Schaap

Sidney Shore, N.Y.C.

Agnus and Doris Day

Rod Warren, N.Y.C.

Creative and Dr. Spock

Larry Pickard, Mamaroneck, N.Y.

Playmate Of The and Senator Carl Mundt

Ron Phlegar, Kew Gardens, N.Y.

Cocoa and Lyle Van

Arthur Penn, Philadelphia, Pa.

Admirable and Soames Forsyte

Robert T. Comey, Plainfield, N.J.

Import and Howdy Doody

Earl Freeman, Utica, N.Y.

Rosy-Fingered and Philip Dorn

Neil D. Isaacs, Knoxville, Tenn.

Painstakingly and Henry David Thoreau

Jonathan Burrows, N.Y.C.

Boats and John Wayne

Gary Carlisle, N.Y.C.

Bedside and Charlie Manna

Margie and Addie Busch, N.Y.C.

The More and Daphne du Maurier

Miles Klein, Belle Harbor, N.Y.

Absolutely and Lionel Trilling

Ruth Passweg, N.Y.C.

Two Cent and Mickey Spillane

Carol Russ, Spring Valley, N.Y.

By Troubles and Jacqueline Bisset

Sam Bassin, Brooklyn, N.Y.

Local and Albert Anastasia

Heavens and Paolo Troubetzkoy

Mrs. Sheldon Berens, N.Y.C.

Ruby and Mel Ott

Rosalie Bernstein, Brooklyn, N.Y.

French and Chita Rivera

Lesley Dormen, N.Y.C.

Ding Dong and Jacques Brel

Jay Begler, East Rockaway, N.Y.

Thor and Martin Luther

Linda Winchester, N.Y.C.

Atchison, Topeka, Santa and Alice Faye

Alice Yohalem, N.Y.C.

Ex and David Hume

Carter Jefferson, Boston, Mass.

Conscientious and Otto Otepka

Newton Brenner, New Haven, Conn.

Hotel and Karl Menninger

Robert M. Hobbs, Philadelphia, Pa.

Immediate and George Seaton

Albert G. Miller, N.Y.C.

Anon and Chester Nimitz

Jim Kent, Alexandria, Va.

Come Up and José Ferrer

Martin E. Healy, Sag Harbor, N.Y.
Charles Mueller, N.Y.C.

Englishmen and Lester Maddox

Walter Lieftl, N.Y.C.

Like Hell and Tom Ewell

Nancy Lowe, N.Y.C.

Epileptic and Sid Caesar

Jerry Richman, N.Y.C.

Third and Theodor Reik

> *Ronda Schiff, N.Y.C.*

Melancholy and Lucius Beebe

> *Sylvia Levine, N.Y.C.*
> *M. Stein, New Haven, Conn.*

Hook Line and Isaac B. Singer

Dais and Irene Dunne

> *Mrs. M. Dingle, Bronx, N.Y.*

A Jury Of One's and Jan Peerce

> *S. A. Carlsson, Yonkers, N.Y.*

Ave Atque and Rudy Vallee

> *Mrs. Paula Van Brink, N.Y.C.*

Irresistible and Lukas Foss

> *James Cohen, West Hartford, Conn.*

Tell Mia and Marie Torre

> *Alix Kaufman, Pittsburgh, Pa.*

Razzle and Denise Darcel

> *Milton Newman, N.Y.C.*

Pop And and Somerset Maugham

> *Mrs. Robert Amft, Evanston, Ill.*

Anything and Harry Goz

> *Meish Goldish, Brooklyn, N.Y.*

A. C. and Eurydice

> *Lucille Bercow, Mamaroneck, N.Y.*

Humpty Dumpty and Barbara Feldon

Thou Shalt Not and Howard Keel

Mrs. A. C. Stanton, Caldwell, N.J.

Roller and George Custer

Erica Anderson, N.Y.C.

Leaving and Vidal Sassoon

Kathryn Wortzel, N.Y.C.
M. Deskey, N.Y.C.

Catfish and Miës van der Rohe

Mari Zipes, N.Y.C.

Gorgon and Emile Zola

Thomas Froncek, N.Y.C.

Standard and Yogi Berra

Colleen Gibbons, Washington, D.C.

T. V. and Joan Diener

William Schlademan, N.Y.C.

Cutting and Chuck Connors

Lorraine Richman, Flushing, N.Y.

Howya and Lorna Doone

William Cole, N.Y.C.

Nina Pinta and Mongo Santamaria

Warren Richmond, Northport, N.Y.

Noah and Cutty Sark

Barry F. Mahl, N.Y.C.

Crash and Alf Landon

Joseph Fisch, New Rochelle, N.Y.

☞ "*Good Fences . . .*"

"Good fences make good neighbors."
—WILLIE SUTTON

Above, a tribute from a stranger. Competitors were invited to submit familiar quotations from unexpected sources.

Repeats: "The way to a man's heart is through his stomach."—DR. CHRISTIAAN BARNARD. "When you are number two you try harder."—S. AGNEW. "I got rhythm."—POPE PAUL. "I never met a man I didn't like."—OSCAR WILDE. "A bird in hand . . ."—L.B.J. "Let them eat cake."—SARA LEE. "I have measured out my life with coffee spoons."—JUAN VALDEZ. "Honor thy father and thy mother."—LIZZIE BORDEN. "You always hurt the one you love."—M. DE SADE. "Neither a borrower nor a lender be."—DAVID ROCKEFELLER. "My cup runneth over."—RACQUEL WELCH. "Speak for yourself, John."—MRS. MARTHA MITCHELL.

"The sweetest sounds I've ever heard are still inside my head."   —LUDWIG VAN BEETHOVEN

"That's funny, you don't look Jewish."   —MAI BRITT
Marvin Aledort, N.Y.C.

"Don't start anything you can't finish."

—FRANZ SCHUBERT

"Let's run it up the flag pole and see who salutes it."

—BETSY ROSS
Marcia Hearst, N.Y.C.

"I hate to cook."

—JOAN OF ARC

"He maketh me to lie down in green pastures."

—LADY CONSTANCE CHATTERLEY
George Grizzard, N.Y.C.

"It's a nice place to visit, but I wouldn't want to live there."

—DANTE ALIGHIERI

"It's a nice place to visit, but I wouldn't want to live there."

—ADAM CLAYTON POWELL
Charlotte Curtis, N.Y.C.

"I have a little shadow that goes in and out with me,
And what can be the use of him is more than I can see."

—RICHARD M. NIXON
Mrs. Neil Brooks, Ashland, Ky.

"Out damned Spot! out, I say!"   —DICK AND JANE*

"Holy smoke!"

—POPE PAUL
Ellen S. Ryp, N.Y.C.
**A. and J. Spielberger, N.Y.C.*
Andrew Herz, N.Y.C.
Edmund Lysek, Chicopee, Mass.
Judith Feder, Brooklyn ,N.Y.

"*Candy* is dandy."   —JUDITH CRIST

"But liquor is quicker."

—CARRIE NATION
Mary Le Mieux, New Orleans, La.

"These are the *Times* that try men's souls."

> —GAY TALESE
>
> *Mrs. Robert Amft, Evanston, Ill.*
> *Bob Lloyd, White Plains, N.Y.*

"Egads and little fishes!" —JACQUES COUSTEAU

"Supercalifragilisticexpialidocious."

> —MARSHALL MCLUHAN
>
> *Gene Oberg, Richmond, Va.*

"It's clever, but is it Art?" —MRS. A. GOLDBERG

"Believe only half of what you see and nothing that you hear."

> —M. DAYAN
>
> *D. Wissel, East Rockaway, N.Y.*

"What would you do if I sang out of tune, would you stand up and walk out on me?"

> —KATHARINE HEPBURN
>
> *Arnold Cover, Sarasota, Fla.*

"Plymouth makes it!"

> —JOHN ALDEN
>
> *Gerald Levy, N.Y.C.*

"Smoking may be hazardous to your health."

> —TONY CURTIS
>
> *Marcia Savage, Lefrak City, N.Y.*
> *N. C. Burg, New Cumberland, Pa.*

"There's many a slip twixt the cup and the lip."

> —ARNOLD PALMER
>
> *M. S. Arentzen, Brooklyn Heights, N.Y.*

"What's in a name?" —ELIZABETH TAYLOR

> HILTON WILDING TODD FISHER BURTON
>
> *Monte Ablin, N.Y.C.*

"What this country needs is a good five-cent cigar."

> —GEORGE SAND
>
> *Rees Behrendt, N.Y.C.*

"Little things mean a lot."   —SNOW WHITE

"United we stand, divided we fall."

—DIANA ROSS AND THE SUPREMES
Arthur J. Cunningham, N.Y.C.

"Share and share alike."

—HERB SARGENT, DAN GREENBURG,
TOM MORROW, *et al.*
Jane W. Norris, N.Y.C.

"What's in a name?"   —ENGLEBERT HUMPERDINCK
Diana Kerew, N.Y.C.

"I Married an Angel."   —EVA BRAUN
Steven Baruch, White Plains, N.Y.

"Hence, vain deluded Joy."

—PROCTOR AND GAMBLE
Mrs. Richard Fein, Brooklyn, N.Y.

"Not responsible for loss of personal property."

—VITO GENOVESE
Judith Kurz, N.Y.C.

"Scouting rounds a guy out."

—GENERAL WESTMORELAND
Joan Kaplan, N.Y.C.

"Dr. Livingstone, I presume?"   —LEWIS AND CLARK
Laurie Quinn, Philadelphia, Pa.

"Don't know why there's no sun up in the sky."

—COPERNICUS
Mrs. Thomas G. Mooney, Asbury Park, N.J.

"I Can't Begin to Tell You."   —HARPO MARX
A. T. Hannett, N.Y.C.
Ruth Neir, Whitestone, N.Y.

"You may fool all the people some of the time; you can even fool some of the people all the time; but you can't fool all of the people all the time."

—RAYMOND MASSEY
Tim Fenton, N.Y.C.

"I'll be a monkey's uncle."

—WILLIAM JENNINGS BRYAN
David Ettinger, N.Y.C.
Sondra Shenkman, N.Y.C.

"To make a long story short . . ."

—MARCEL PROUST
Michael Deskey, N.Y.C.

"Sighted sub, sank same."

—CHRISTOPHER COLUMBUS
T. L. Shelley, White Plains, N.Y.

"I'm nobody! Who are you? Are you nobody, too?"

—TRUMAN CAPOTE
Deborah Schwabach, Wilmington, Del.

"How do I love thee? Let me count the ways."

—KRAFFT-EBING
Arthur Penn, Philadelphia, Pa.

"Thank God it's Friday."   —ROBINSON CRUSOE
Nora Johnson, Wynnewood, Pa.

"Accuracy, accuracy, accuracy."   —WILLIAM TELL
George Flynn, Jr., Dallas, Tex.

"There is no tomorrow."   —HUGH DOWNS
Mrs. James M. Herron, St. Louis, Mo.

"Into each life a little rain must fall."

—BURT BACHARACH
Charles Neerland, Edina, Minn.

"He who enjoys a good neighbor has a precious posses-
sion."   —BOB, CAROL, TED, AND ALICE
                            Robert M. Brandt, St. Clair Shores, Mich.

". . . Never send to know for whom the bell tolls."
                                                          —PAVLOV
                                      J. Jeffery Leimsieder, N.Y.C.

"A is for Apple."   —MISS HESTER PRYNNE
                            Cynthia Brown, Garden City, N.Y.

"Over the river and through the wood,
   now Grandmother's cap I spy!
Hurrah for the fun! Is the pudding done?
   Hurrah for the pumpkin pie!"
                            —HUGH HEFNER AND BERNIE CORNFELD
                                   Addie Salzberg, Brooklyn, N.Y.

"I Led Three Lives."   —DONALD DUCK
                            Larry E. Boram, Pendleton, Ind.

"Where there's a will, there's a way."
                                              —MRS. BILLY ROSE
                            Barbara Kleinman, Brooklyn, N.Y.

"You're sick, sick, sick."   —MARY BAKER EDDY
                                        Albert Miller, N.Y.C.

☞ My Kitty
Likes Ballet . . .

My kitty likes ballet (entrechat), movies (Fe-line-I), poetry (Pusskin), music (Caterina Va-lente), and education (Nathan Pusey). She is Catholic, wears purple, drinks Muscatel, and lives in Washington Mews. In summer, I whisker away to my chateau in Pawling, N.Y. When she is tired I give my catatonic or apply mouse-to-mouse re-suscitation. Who steals my puss does not steal trash. I love my cat. (But, oh, you Kitt!)

Above, a supposed composition by pun-loving Bennett Cerf, age eight. Competitors were invited to submit a brief essay on "My Pet" as written in the style of any well-known person, age eight, about his or her favorite animal. (Limit seventy-five words.)

MY PET

My hound dog, Moriarty, was found one foggy night ly-ing near death in a copse of copper beeches. Around his neck was clasped a speckled band from which depended a miniature violin case containing a strange white powder. The local constable, P. C. Lestrade, reported having seen him earlier in the company of a red-headed man and a filthy lascar. My friend, John Watson, and I doctored him with poultices of shag tobacco, and then we turned on.　　　　　　　　　　　　　　—S. HOLMES

Joyce Harrington, Brooklyn, N.Y.

THE OLD CHOW GAME

Every kind of person keeps a pet. This is a very human kind of thing to do. Some of them are poor people. Downtown, there are a few, maybe ten, maybe a dozen guys who wear silk suits and drink good Scotch, and they buy up the waste meat products (my friend Normy says) and they can it for pet food. This is not such a human thing to do. Thirty cents a can is what they're getting.

—JIMMY BRESLIN

Edwin Ahearn, Brooklyn, N.Y.

MY PET

My dog's name is SPOT. He's TOPS. He chases my sister's cat, Punctuation, around the POST. Once they had a fight in the kitchen and upset the POTS. "STOP, SPOT," I said. "Ignore Punctuation."

—RICHARD MALTBY, JR.

Arnold Cover, Sarasota, Fla.

MY CAT IN SEVENTY-FIVE WORDS

I would say, clarifying at the outset that my opinion is colored by love and does not attempt to claim any validity as an objective truth, that my cat, whom (I use the word whom rather than which with the full knowledge that many will accuse me of being anthropomorphic which, in this case and ironically enough, is precisely the meaning I wish to convey) I have not previously acknowledged, to any degree, on the written page, due most directly to the fact that I acquired my writing skills only a scant two years ago despite the prodigious efforts of my elder brother William, who most doggedly attempted, to no avail, to instruct me in penmanship at the age of three, is a remarkable animal, combining not only the grace, but the intuitive sense of dignity and femininity as well as a high intelligence most often associated with those European women who, like the great Madame du Châtelet, the mistress of that French master of the satiric style, Voltaire, so captivated the cultivated world of the eighteenth century, with a vivacity, freshness and, above all, in fact, really, encompassing the previous two adjectives, an innocence that I must, and can only, having not yet had the opportunity for much travel, being confined to what I may call, with absolute truth in regard to myself, though others might reprimand me for a somewhat autocratic attitude, which would, in a larger sense, be a just criticism, my home, classify as uniquely American.

—HENRY JAMES
Janice Brophy, N.Y.C.

MY PET
Dog.

—CALVIN COOLIDGE
Fred Cline, N.Y.C.

MY PET
How did I get my dog Spot? I got Spot bcause my parents gave him to me because I made my bed every day this last summer. What kind of dog is Spot? Spot is dark brown, with white patches. He has short furry legs, and one ear is flopped over. He had a very small tail and he is a son of a bitch.

—JERRY RUBIN
Andrew Berkman, N.Y.C.

OUR PET
My brother and I love our wolf. She is like a mother to us. I think we are too old for this sort of pet. But I always say, "When with Romulus, do as Romulus does." Next week my brother wants to spend a day building a city. He wants to name it Reme, after me. Ha, ha. He kills me. I must go now. I hear the dinner bark.

—REMUS
Donald Wigal, N.Y.C.

MY PET

My pet has yellow feathers, eats lots of bird food, and lives in a cage. (Joey chews gum in class.) He likes to hop around inside his cage. I don't think he would like to get out. (Louise smokes in the boys' room.) At night I put a cover over his cage. When I take the cover off in the morning, he sings and sings and sings. (Paul steals at the five-and-ten.)　　　　　　　—JOE VALACHI

James F. Graham, N.Y.C.

MY KITTY

My kitty is brown with yellow stripes. My kitty had three babies yesterday. If each of the baby kittens has three babies next year, we will have nine babies. In twenty years, we will have 2,636,541,171 baby kittens. My friend Janie, next door, also has a kitty.

　　　　　　　—MARGARET SANGER

Joseph T. Rigo, N.Y.C.

MY SECRET FRIEND

My secret friend is an animal. Whenever I have a party I ride him, feed him, and pat his head. I like running with him but it's all very secret because he belongs mostly to Edmund, Harold, Teddy, Eugene, and one part to Hubie. I wish I could buy him but I think the price is too high. Maybe when I grew up, around 1972, I will have enough. Especially if I sell my elephant.　　　—JOHN LINDSAY

Marvin Goodman, N.Y.C.

FAT CAT

all dressed in black with spotsofwhite
proud to defend whatsyours with fight.
huge almondeyes of sparkling yellowgreen
lookingandwatching what haveyouseen?
you sitandbe with a wisdom of longago
where haveyoubeen what doyouknow?

but wont ever tell will you
sillypusscatominesillyou
SCOOBY DOO!

—E. E. CUMMINGS
Henrietta Lizewski, N.Y.C.

MY PET(S) QUINTETTE

INSTRUCTIONS: The puzzle consists of five diminutive
words that are related to a sixth word that is related to a
seventh word.

1. Ram X Ewe (4 letters)
2. One type of market (4 letters)
3. The one that came first crossed the road (3 letters)
4. The fog walks on her feet (3 letters)
5. Goes with chips (4 letters)
6. Bobby, bubbi, baby's celebration (8 letters)
7. You let her entertain you (5 letters)

—STEPHEN SONDHEIM
Martin Meyers, N.Y.C.

MY PET

Not fur. Not crawling. Not swimming. Not on the lawn.
Pigeon is a pigeon is a pigeon. This subject does not in-
terest me today. —GERTRUDE STEIN
Barbara L. Michaels, Red Hook, N.Y.

MY PET

O my pet has the eye of a braw lord, and the lug of a
birkie. He oft gae in for fits o' daffin. The moving why I
luv him so be tha' he and I are so the same. He is not
coof, and to me he is worth all the gawd in the world,
Yestreen when he and I walked thru the heather to see us
would hae ta'en ye fancy. —ROBERT BURNS
Marie Stecklare, Burlington, Vt.

MY DOGGIE

I love pets. Take my dog—please. When I was a little kid
we were too poor to have a dog, so my brother and I

bought a leash and took turns walking each other. But we never stopped hoping; we even saved up fleas just in case. Now I have a dog who likes to play outside in the mud and then run around the house. Every night I say, "Goodnight, Swamp." Wouldn't you rather have me stay after school and play my violin for you?

—HENNY YOUNGMAN
Martin Schlesinger, N.Y.C.

MY PET BULL
Was late for school (Yoknapatawpha Elementary, all white) having taken, coaxed, tricked my pet bull to the cow (bequeathed to my sister Caddy—doomed and knew it—by Col. Sartoris who failed at Shiloh) so Teacher asked me why Daddy hadn't done it and when I replied, was bound to reply, my bull could do it better, Teacher talked himself voiceless while I watched with hope (and then even hope died) his hand holding the cane.

—WILLIAM FAULKNER
F. Harry Brown, N.Y.C.

MY PET
She is tall, brunette, naked, and mine, all mine. Such games we play! First she whips me, then I whip her. After *déjeuner* she straps me into bed for my nap and lulls me to sleep with gentle screams of terror. Later I attach her black-leather halter and take her for a walk through *Grand-mère's* barbecue pit. For my birthday, Papa has promised a special treat: I am going to kill her.

—M. DE SADE
George Malko, N.Y.C.

MY PET
I have a cat. And that's that.

—THEODORE (DR. SEUSS) GEISEL
Jerald Silverman, Pearl River, N.Y.

STYTH

Styth, a Fulgabian zwobix, is my pet. What is a zwobix, you ask? It is a creature with three legs, like a stool (the back one disappears when it walks); two bright blue eyes, and two yellow ones which open up after the sun goes down; and long hair everywhere except for its head which is covered with red scales. It smells like a cantaloupe and says "greep, greep." Zwobi are kind and very obedient.
                                               —J. R. R. TOLKIEN
                                     Arthur Penn, Philadelphia, Pa.

MY PET

Who are you, and what makes you think that I have a pet?
                                               —SOCRATES
                                     Paul J. Brinson, Kenmore, N.Y.

MY PET

My pet Pixie is naughty. I saw Pixie kiss another dog; that's naughty. He tried to run away from me yesterday; that's naughty. He won't do what I tell him to do; that's naughty. If he stays naughty I will kill him.

                                               —RONA BARRETT
                                     David Yarnell, N.Y.C.

MY PET

Let me make it clear, my hawk is a dovelike bird. I did not originate this bird, I inherited it. But I am its owner, let there be no mistaking that. . . .

                                               —RICHARD NIXON
                                     Michael Schreiber, Brooklyn, N.Y.

MY PET

I'm going to tell you about my favorite pet. He's an excellent pet and I'm sure you'll enjoy hearing about him. My pet is a dog named Spiro. I once tried to teach him to fetch my slippers but he always went after the newspaper instead. He liked to rip the newspaper apart, maybe because he was always hit in the snout by a newspaper. Now he's very vicious so I try to muzzle him.

—RICHARD NIXON
Jeffrey A. Wurst, Hempstead, N.Y.

MY PET

My pet is a goldfish. I won my goldfish in the Wool-worth's Goldfish Essay Contest. Then I took my goldfish home and my mother fed it matzoh balls and I won the Fattest Goldfish Contest. Then I put my goldfish on a starvation diet and won the Skinniest Goldfish Contest. Then I took my goldfish to school and won the School Show and Tell Contest. Then I bred my goldfish with another goldfish and won the Goldfish Breeding Contest. Next week is the Goldfish Eating Contest and I plan to win that too. But don't worry. Right after that the kids on the block are holding a Barfing Contest.

—DAN GREENBURG
Peter Hochstein, N.Y.C.

MY PET

Last night my parents gave me a parakeet. Why they did this is beyond me. It is ridiculously tiny, and appears to be a mouse with feathers. It nips me whenever I put a hand in its cage. Its vocabulary is pitifully small, and its diction leaves much to be desired. It feeds on the most woeful seeds. My parents as recently as eight years ago were able to produce something as notable as myself. Surely they could do better in choosing a pet.

—JOHN SIMON
Pericles Crystal, Brooklyn, N.Y.

MY PET

. . . My cat sits looking over harbor and city on silent haunches and then moves on . . . sometimes it comes in on little pet feet.   —CARL SANDBURG
Ann Lipman, N.Y.C.

MYN PETTE

Myn slepyng hound is broun,
His smale tale is doun;
Wel loves he bouns and scrappes,
Strong wyn and myghty ale he lappes.
This noble dogge has gentil herte,
Smale foweles he taken aparte.
His barke is loude, his tooth is longe,
He kisses myn face with his sweete tonge.
For the proverbe seith that
"He is gentil that dooth gentil thynges,"
Up roos myn slepyng hound
And to me brighte joly love he brynges.

—GEOFFREY CHAUCER
Paul Noble, N.Y.C.